Preface

The world in which we live is a place where things are always changing. These changes can sometimes happen rather suddenly, while at other times they transpire over many, many years. Regardless of the time it takes for change to happen, without a keen understanding of the culture and history that generates change, it can sometimes be impossible to understand why things transpire the way they do. It is with these thoughts in mind that we set out to create a textbook for Japanese English as a foreign language learners that we believe will help learners to not only improve at English, but to also learn more about one particular society's culture that has often captivated the world—American culture.

While it was not easy to select material from the abundance of cultural information that is available on America, we believe that the 15 units that comprise this book will be diverse enough to at least pique interest into a portion of all seven elements that make up a single culture. Moreover, each unit is comprised of two readings on a given theme, with one of the readings presenting information on the historical significance of a topic, and the other offering readers a more current perspective or popular trend. As for the pedagogical merits of this textbook, we have structured each unit in the following manner: Each unit will begin with a couple of warmup questions that are meant to stimulate discussions on the unit themes. In addition, there are some scaffolding-type exercises for each of the reading passages that will aid in vocabulary learning. Following each reading, there are some multiple choice and true-or-false reading comprehension questions. Furthermore, the second reading passage contains a listening comprehension section, and some word order exercises after each reading passage can be used to help with English grammar comprehension.

We would like to thank all those who have contributed to the development of this book, both directly and indirectly, and we would like to extend a special thanks to our editors, Yukiko Mori and Keiko Nagano and our publisher, Shouhakusha. We hope this textbook finds favor with students and teachers who want to study English and learn more about American culture. May the stories be inspiring, educational, and most of all, interesting enough to make you want to become better at English and learn more about what makes America so American.

The Authors

Modern America:
Culture, Society and History

Contents

© dani3315 / Shutterstock.com

Chapter 1

America's Easter Tradition

イースターの慣習

> イースターは、クリスマスのように決まった日ではないことを知っていますか？ 毎年最も早い日で 3 月 22 日、最も遅い日で 4 月 25 日の日曜日がイースターの日になります。それでは、米国のイースターの慣習について読んでみましょう。

Reading 1 ▶ Warm-up

Using your dictionary, find the meanings of the following words.

1. celebrate
2. resurrection
3. tradition
4. officially
5. attend
6. fancy
7. organize
8. traffic

Choose the best answer (a-c).

1. What is the most important holiday for American Christians?

   a. Christmas
   b. Easter
   c. Jesus Christ

2. What does the word "participants" mean?

   a. Christians
   b. rich people
   c. partakers

Reading 1   The Easter Parade

1 Easter is the most important holiday for Christians in America because it celebrates the death and resurrection of Jesus Christ. However, because of Easter traditions like the Easter Bunny, Easter eggs, Easter candy, and the Easter Parade, Easter is a major holiday
5   that is celebrated by both Christians and non-Christians in the USA.

2 Although many Easter traditions found their way to America from other countries, one tradition that is uniquely American is the Easter Parade. The Easter Parade began in New York City in the mid-1800s. The exact start of the parade is unknown because it was not an officially
10 organized event until the 20th century. On Fifth Avenue in New York City, there are various churches that were attended by the rich in the mid-1800s, and on Easter, the people who attended these churches would go to Easter church services wearing new and fancy clothes and hats. Then, after church services were finished, the rich would all leave
15 their churches at the same time and walk down Fifth Avenue. All of these fancy and expensive clothes soon attracted average citizens who would gather to watch all of the fanciness.

3 Today, the New York City Easter Parade is an organized event that results in Fifth Avenue being closed to traffic from 49th Street to 57th
20 Street during the day. Participants in this parade, like in the past, often wear very fancy hats. Also, because of the New York City Easter Parade tradition, other cities in America also have their own Easter parades.

NOTES
l. 10: **Avenue** 南北に走る通り > Street は東西を走る通り

Comprehension Questions

Choose the best answer (a-c).

1. Why is Easter an important holiday for Christians in America?

   a. Because they want to celebrate the Easter bunny

   b. Because they want to celebrate the Easter Parade

   c. Because they hope to celebrate what happened to Jesus Christ

2. Which is NOT an Easter tradition?

   a. The Easter Bunny

   b. The Easter Chicken

   c. Easter candy

3. Who were the original Easter Parade participants?

   a. People with lots of money

   b. People who recently came to America

   c. People who didn't like going to church

4. What did rich people wear for Easter in the mid-1800s?

   a. Cheap clothes

   b. Plain hats

   c. New clothes

5. When did the Easter Parade become an organized event?

   a. In the 1900s

   b. During the 19th century

   c. Within the last 20 years

6. Why did common people want to look at rich people after they left church on Easter?

   a. Because they wore interesting clothes

   b. Because they smelled so nice

   c. Because they looked like the average citizen

7. Which is the street where the Easter Parade is held today?

   a. 49th Street

   b. 5th Avenue

   c. 57th Street

T/F Questions

Circle T or F for each of the following statements.

1. The Easter Parade is a celebration that started because of traditions from other countries. (**T** / **F**)

2. Rich New Yorkers liked to exchange hats during the Easter Parade. (**T** / **F**)

3. Easter parades are only held in New York City. (**T** / **F**)

Writing Questions

Make a full sentence, using the following words.

1. The Easter Parade (America / is / started / that / a tradition / in) over 150 years ago.

_____

2. (Fancy / are / worn / for / hats / commonly) the Easter Parade.

_____

Reading 2 **Listening**

Listen to the following "Reading 2." Fill in the correct word or phrase in each blank (a-e) and match the definitions below.

a. _____ b. _____ c. _____

d. _____ e. _____

1. candy
2. is connected with something
3. an instrument
4. a newcomer to a country
5. a type of potato chip
6. a newly born bird
7. is very popular

Reading 2 Easter Candy

After Halloween, Easter is the second **(a)** candy holiday in America, and the sweets that are the most popular among Americans for the Easter holiday are chocolate eggs. Interestingly, eggs have been associated with Easter since the early 19th century in Europe. A uniquely American egg-shaped candy is the jellybean, which became **(b)** Easter in the 1930s. 5 According to the National Confectioners Association, over 16 billion jellybeans are made in the U.S. each year for Easter, enough to fill a giant egg measuring 89 feet high and 60 feet wide. Since the turn of the century, the top-selling non-chocolate Easter candy has been the marshmallow Peep, a sugary, pastel-colored **(c)**. Peeps were created by 10 Sam Born, a Russian **(d)** who came to America from France and founded a candy manufacturing company called Just Born. The original Peeps that were sold in the 1950s were handmade, marshmallow-flavored yellow **(e)**, but there are now Peeps that are sold in many different shapes and flavors, including chocolate mousse bunnies. 15

NOTES
l. 6: **the National Confectioners Association** 全米菓子協会   l. 6: **billion** 1億   l. 8: **feet** 1フィートは約30.48cm

Comprehension Questions

Choose the best answer (a-c).

1. What American holiday has the most candy sales?

    a. Easter

    b. Halloween

    c. Christmas

2. What is the most popular Easter candy?

    a. Chocolate eggs

    b. Chocolate mousse bunnies

    c. Jellybeans

3. Since when have eggs been associated with Easter?

    a. Since the early 19th century

    b. Since the 1930s

    c. Since the 1950s

4. How many jellybeans are sold in the US each year?

    a. 89 thousand

    b. More than 16 billion

    c. Almost 19 billion

5. What is the most popular non-chocolate Easter candy?

    a. Jellybeans

    b. Giant eggs

    c. Peeps

6. What color were the Peeps that Sam Born's company made in the 1950s?

    a. Brown

    b. Yellow

    c. Chocolate

7. What is the birthplace of Sam Born?

    a. Russia

    b. France

    c. America

T/F Questions

Circle T or F for each of the following statements.

1. Peeps were originally made from chocolate mousse. (**T** / **F**)

2. The first Peeps looked like baby chickens. (**T** / **F**)

3. Jellybeans are no longer sold in the US. (**T** / **F**)

Writing Questions

Make a full sentence, using the following words.

1. The candy that (Americans / Easter / eat / at / the most / is) the chocolate egg.

_____

2. Peeps (popular / the / most / second / are / candy) that is sold for Easter in America.

_____

Chapter 2

America's Inner-city Music

インナーシティ・ミュージック

> 「インナーシティ」はアメリカ独自の用語です。必ずしもダウンタウンや都市の中心部を意味するわけではなく、貧困層、黒人、都市部の近隣を意味する場合が多く、音楽のようにこれらの地域から生まれたもの、あるいはこれらの地域で起こるものを表現するために使われます。

Reading 1 ▶ ## Warm-up

Using your dictionary, find the meanings of the following words.

1. immigrate	**2.** develop	**3.** set	**4.** emulate
5. observation	**6.** rhythm	**7.** trace	**8.** demonstrate

Choose the best answer (a-c).

1. What popular American music has its roots in Jamaican music?

   a. Rock and roll

   b. Country music

   c. Hip hop

2. What does the word "spinning" mean?

   a. dancing

   b. playing

   c. singing

Reading 1　Hip Hop

🔊 Audio 04

1 Hip hop is a style of music that was born in America. It is said that the father of hip hop is DJ Kool Herc. DJ Kool Herc's real name is Clive Campbell. He was born in Jamaica, but at the age of 10, he and his family immigrated to America. During Clive's teenage years, he began to develop the hip hop style. It was in the early 1970s that Clive began ⁵ spinning records at parties and between sets when his father's band performed. DJ Kool Herc often emulated the style of Jamaican DJs by "toasting" (i.e., talking) over the records that he played.

2 DJ Kool Herc was very skilled at observation. By observation, he learned that people would wait for particular parts of a record to be ¹⁰ played before they would dance, and it was often that the dancing would occur during times when the vocals would stop and there would be drum rhythms. As a result, DJ Kool Herc decided to use two turntables that would play the same music. By doing this, he could switch back and forth between the two records and have the drum parts play for longer. ¹⁵ This technique is called "break beat."

3 As for the date when hip hop was born, it can be traced to a birthday party that was held in New York City on August 11th, 1973. The birthday girl was Clive Campbell's sister. For her party, Clive got to demonstrate for a large birthday party audience his break-beat style and ²⁰ skills that he developed that year. It was the success of the birthday party that led to the birth of hip hop music.

NOTES
l. 10: **particular** 特定の、こだわりの　ll. 14-15: **back and forth** 前後に

Comprehension Questions

Choose the best answer (a-c).

1. Who is DJ Kool Herc?

   a. The man who invented the turntable

   b. The most famous break dancer

   c. An American immigrant who created hip hop music

2. What is NOT true about Clive Campbell?

   a. He was born in America.

   b. He used two turntables.

   c. He played music at the same places as his father.

3. When did DJ Kool Herc start to develop his style?

   a. When he was in Jamaica

   b. When he was in his teens

   c. After his sister's birthday

4. What music hip hop technique is from Jamaica?

   a. Talking over records

   b. Using two turntables

   c. Dancing during drum rhythms

5. Why did DJ Kool Herc use two turntables?

   a. Because he wanted to play the music louder

   b. Because he wanted people to dance more

   c. Because it was popular with Jamaican DJs

6. When was hip hop born in America?

   a. At a birthday party

   b. Between sets when Clive's father's band performed

   c. When Clive arrived in America

7. Where did hip hop begin in America?

   a. In Jamaica

   b. In New York

   c. In Clive's father's hometown

T/F Questions

Circle T or F for each of the following statements.

1. People who listened to DJ Kool Herc liked dancing when there was singing. (**T** / **F**)

2. "Break beat" is when a DJ uses two records to repeat a part of a song. (**T** / **F**)

3. Clive Campbell is said to be the godfather of hip hop. (**T** / **F**)

Writing Questions

Make a full sentence, using the following words.

1. Hip hop is (a / that / of / people / music / style) like dancing to.

   _____

2. At a birthday party, Clive Campbell (and / became / started / famous / the) hip hop style of music.

   _____

© pisaphotography / Shutterstock.com

Listen to the following "Reading 2." Fill in the correct word or phrase in each blank (a-e) and match the definitions below.

a. _____   b. _____   c. _____

d. _____   e. _____

1. popularity

2. stored

3. talented

4. poor

5. difficult

6. a person who is not honest

7. a person who writes stories

Reading 2 ▸ Kendrick Lamar

In April 2018, Kendrick Lamar Duckworth became the first person to win a Pulitzer Prize for a hip-hop album. The people who chose Kendrick Lamar for a Pulitzer Prize said that his music had a unique and powerful rhythm that expressed to listeners the **(a)** lives that African Americans
5 live. The lyrics of some of his songs tell listeners of his youth, being black, poor, and **(b)**. In addition to winning a Pulitzer Prize, Kendrick Lamar has sold more than 17 million albums, he has been nominated for 29 Grammys, he has won 12 Grammys, and his work is **(c)** at Harvard University's library. His **(d)** has brought him the title of poet laureate of
10 hip-hop, and his skillful storytelling has resulted in him being compared to **(e)** James Joyce and James Baldwin. His storytelling began when he was a child growing up in Compton, California. After writing stories as a child, he began to write poems, and then lyrics, which he put to music. It was in 2003 when he was 16 years old that he got his break. His mixtape
15 was discovered by the hip-hop producer Dr. Dre and with Dr. Dre's help, he went on to become the star that he is today.

NOTES　l. 2: **Pulitzer Prize** 1917 年に創設され米国内の新聞、雑誌、オンラインの報道などの功績に対し与えられる賞。
l. 7: **million** 100 万　l. 9: **poet laureate** 桂冠詩人 (優れた詩人に与えられる称号)

Comprehension Questions

Choose the best answer (a-c).

1. When did Kendrick Lamar win a Pulitzer Prize?
   a. When he was 16
   b. In 2003
   c. In April 2018

2. How many people have won a Pulitzer Prize for a hip-hop album?
   a. 1 person
   b. 12 people
   c. 29 people

3. What is NOT a theme in Kendrick Lamar's lyrics?
   a. Being an African American
   b. Growing up with no money
   c. Having no talent

4. When did Kendrick Lamar begin writing stories?
   a. When he was a child
   b. When he was a teenager
   c. After becoming an adult

5. Whose writing is Kendrick Lamar's storytelling like?
   a. Dr. Dre
   b. James Joyce
   c. James Compton

6. What did Kendrick Lamar write before he began writing poems?
   a. Rap songs
   b. Lyrics
   c. Stories

7. How old was Kendrick Lamar when he got his break?
   a. 12 years old
   b. 16 years old
   c. 17 years old

T/F Questions

Circle T or F for each of the following statements.

1. Harvard University keeps copies of Kendrick Lamar's lyrics in their library. (**T** / **F**)

2. Lamar was a famous musical star before he met Dr. Dre. (**T** / **F**)

3. Kendrick Lamar's early music was recorded on CDs. (**T** / **F**)

Writing Questions

Make a full sentence, using the following words.

1. Because of Kendrick Lamar's talent, (hip-hop / of / has been called / the / he / poet laureate).

   _____

2. Not (for / he / only / nominated / been / has) 29 Grammy awards, but Kendrick Lamar has also won 12 Grammys.

   _____

Chapter 3

African American Music

アフリカ系アメリカ人の音楽

> アフリカ系アメリカ人の音楽の初期の形態は、西アフリカに由来するもので、アフリカから米国に連れてこられた奴隷によって伝えられました。米国にきた当時の奴隷たちは、ドラムや木琴、バンジョーなどの楽器に精通していたのです。

Reading 1 ▶ **Warm-up**

Using your dictionary, find the meanings of the following words.

1. evolve	**2.** lyric	**3.** reflect	**4.** urban
5. rural	**6.** dramatic	**7.** transition	**8.** ensemble

Choose the best answer (a-c).

1. What does the word "genre" mean?

   a. kind

   b. place

   c. people

2. What genre of music was born as a result of migrating to cities in the U.S.?

   a. The blues

   b. R&B

   c. Boogie-woogie

🔊 Audio 06

1 Rhythm and Blues, commonly known as R&B, is a unique genre of African American music that has evolved from many other forms of African American music, such as the blues, swing, gospel, and boogie-woogie. What is more, the lyrics tell the complex stories of African American life experiences and continue to reflect changes in American society, culture, and urban life. Furthermore, the development of R&B is closely related with the growth of twentieth-century African American urban communities in cities such as Chicago, Los Angeles, New York, Memphis, and Detroit.

2 The early development of R&B happened between 1941 and 1950, when many African Americans moved from the Southern and rural regions of the United States to Northern cities to work in factories that needed industrial workers. As a result of these dramatic changes in population from rural to urban, not only was African American music able to transition from rural to urban centers, but the growth of African American communities in urban centers led to the development of large audiences of African Americans who had money and desired social interaction with music and entertainment. As a result of this social and economic change in America, the timing was perfect for the blending of musicians, musical experimentation, and the birth of R&B.

3 Throughout the history of R&B, there are many sounds that people have come to associate with this genre of music. That is, R&B is made up of a range of musical characteristics, instrumentation, and ensembles. The size of R&B groups ranged from small piano trios to large groups. Some large groups could even contain full rhythm and horn sections. Notably, R&B was performed with acoustic instruments in the 1940s but was "plugged in" and made electric from the late 1950s.

NOTES
l. 23: **instrumentation** 器楽編成法

Comprehension Questions

Choose the best answer (a-c).

1. What music did NOT form a part of R&B?

   a. Swing

   b. Hip hop

   c. Gospel

2. What is unique about R&B music?

   a. It became famous in rural America.

   b. It tells about what African Americans are going through.

   c. The sound is always the same.

3. Why did many African Americans move to cities in the 1940s?

   a. Because they wanted to become musicians

   b. Because they hoped to work in factories

   c. Because they wanted to hear R&B music

4. What change in America lead to the early development of R&B?

   a. There was a major population shift in the 1940s.

   b. There was a decline in storytelling in big cities.

   c. African Americans wanted to become more international.

5. What is NOT true of African American factory workers in the 1940s?

   a. They wanted to meet people and listen to music.

   b. They hoped for economic support.

   c. They had enough money to enjoy music.

6. What led to the birth of R&B in the 1940s?

   a. The development of acoustical and electric instruments

   b. A change in the economies and communities of urban centers

   c. The growth of urban and rural centers

7. After the 1950s, what happened to R&B music?

   a. Musicians stopped making R&B music with acoustic instruments.

   b. The size of R&B groups grew smaller for a time.

   c. Horn sections were added to the music for the first time.

T/F Questions

Circle T or F for each of the following statements.

1. Many African Americans wanted to gather together to listen to music between 1941 and 1950. (**T** / **F**)

2. R&B has one unique sound that people associate with this genre of music. (**T** / **F**)

3. The sound of R&B music is very limited. (**T** / **F**)

Writing Questions

Make a full sentence, using the following words.

1. R&B music is a (created / African / by / music / that / was) Americans.

   _____

2. (a / the / 1940s / of / were / time) dramatic change in America.

   _____

© Anton_Ivanov / Shutterstock.com

Reading 2 ▶ Listening

Audio 07

> Listen to the following "Reading 2." Fill in the correct word or phrase in each blank (a-e) and match the definitions below.

a. ▭▭▭▭▭▭   b. ▭▭▭▭▭▭   c. ▭▭▭▭▭▭

d. ▭▭▭▭▭▭   e. ▭▭▭▭▭▭

1. to invent something new
2. to participate
3. chosen
4. stop being a group
5. to remake for a new purpose
6. first
7. to begin a new relationship

Reading 2 ▷ Beyoncé

Beyoncé Giselle Knowles was born in Houston, Texas on September 4, 1981. She started singing at an early age and entered her first talent show at age 7, singing John Lennon's *Imagine*. She went on **(a)** in and win many talent shows after her **(b)**. Beyoncé Knowles became famous around the world after she started performing as the lead vocalist for   5
the R&B group Destiny's Child. After Destiny's Child **(c)**, Beyoncé began a solo career with her debut album *Dangerously in Love* and soon became one of music's top-selling R&B artists. As of 2020, Beyoncé has won 24 Grammy Awards and has been **(d)** for 70, which makes her the most nominated woman in history. Beyoncé has also starred in several 10
films, including *Dreamgirls*, which was **(e)** from the hit Broadway musical. In 2008, she married hip-hop recording artist Jay-Z. The couple has three children. Their oldest daughter, Blue Ivy Carter was born in 2012 and sings with her mother, Saint Jhn, and Wizkid in *Brown Skin Girl*.   15

NOTES   l. 9: **Grammy Awards** ザ・レコーディング・アカデミーが主催し 1958 年に開始した。音楽界では世界最高峰の音楽賞の一つとされ、毎年行なわれる授賞式は著名なアーティストが出演し、多くの国で放映される。

Comprehension Questions

1. Where was Beyoncé born?

    a. Houston, Texas

    b. Broadway

    c. Hollywood

2. How old was Beyoncé when she entered her first talent show?

    a. Four

    b. Seven

    c. Twelve

3. What song did Beyoncé sing at her first talent show?

    a. *Imagine*

    b. *Dangerously in Love*

    c. *Dreamgirls*

4. When did Beyoncé begin her solo career?

    a. After her debut album

    b. After her marriage to Jay-Z

    c. After leaving Destiny's Child

5. How many times has Beyoncé been nominated for a Grammy Award?

    a. Seven times

    b. Seventeen times

    c. Seventy times

6. How many women have been nominated for more Grammy Awards than Beyoncé?

    a. None

    b. One

    c. Several

7. What film did Beyoncé star in that was first a Broadway musical?

    a. *Goldengirls*

    b. *Dreamgirls*

    c. *Destiny's Girls*

T/F Questions

1. Beyoncé's middle name is giraffe. (**T** / **F**)

2. Beyoncé and Jay-Z's daughter was named after a color. (**T** / **F**)

3. The song *Brown Skin Girl* was sung by Beyoncé and three others. (**T** / **F**)

Writing Questions

Make a full sentence, using the following words.

1. Beyoncé Giselle Knowles married Jay-Z (years / was / old / she / 26 / when).

   _____

2. Beyoncé and her daughter both sang in the song *Brown Skin Girl*, (which / from / song / is / a) *The Lion King* movie.

   _____

© S-F / Shutterstock.com

The American Academy of Motion Picture Arts and Sciences

映画技術科学アカデミー

" なぜロサンゼルスが「世界のエンターテイメントの都」と呼ばれている
か知っていますか？　それは、ロサンゼルスの一帯であるハリウッドで
多くの映画が作られていること、そして米国の映画やテレビの産業がロ
サンゼルスを拠点としていることに由来しています。"

Reading 1 ▶ Warm-up

Using your dictionary, find the meanings of the following words.

1. outstanding   2. informally   3. sculpture   4. knight

5. film reel   6. symbolic   7. statuette   8. extravagant

Choose the best answer (a-c).

1. What is something that actors and actresses likely hope to receive at least once in their lifetimes?
   a. An Oscar
   b. A Grammy
   c. A Superbowl

2. What does the word "branch" mean?
   a. club
   b. membership
   c. discipline

Reading 1 ▸ The Academy Awards

🔊 Audio 08

1 In 1929, the Academy of Motion Picture Arts and Sciences, located in Beverly Hills, California, began giving out awards for outstanding work to people in the film industry. The awards ceremony, formally called the Academy Awards and informally the Oscars from 1939, began by only giving out 12 awards to men and women who worked in one of the 5 following film branches: acting, directing, producing, writing, and technical. Today, however, the number of available Academy Awards has increased to 23. The trophy that the winners receive is a sculpture that is approximately 34 centimeters tall and weighs 3.8 kilograms. The trophy, usually called an Oscar, is of a knight holding a sword while 10 standing on a film reel. Interestingly, the film reel has five spokes, which are symbolic of each of the Academy's original five film branches.

2 So why do people like to call the sculpture an Oscar and the awards the Oscars? While it is unclear why people like the nickname so much, the origin has been narrowed down to three possible sources. The most 15 accepted story comes from the belief that a librarian who worked at the Academy of Motion Picture Arts and Sciences said that the statuette looked like her uncle Oscar. Another belief is that a newspaper writer made up the nickname for the trophy to make the awards sound less extravagant. Lastly, it has also been said that when Bette Davis won the 20 award for Best Actress, she said that the backside of the trophy looked like her husband Harmon Oscar Nelson. Whatever the cause of the popularity for the nickname, the Oscars are likely to remain popular with film industry workers and fans for many years to come.

NOTES
l. 9: **approximately** 約、およそ　l. 10: **sword** 剣

Comprehension Questions

Choose the best answer (a-c).

1. When did the Academy Awards begin giving out awards to directors?

    a. 1929
    b. 1934
    c. 1939

2. How many Academy awards were given out in 1929?

    a. 12
    b. 24
    c. 34

3. What is NOT true about the Academy Awards trophy?

    a. It is holding a weapon.
    b. It is 340 millimeters tall.
    c. It looks like a tree with only five branches.

4. Why does the film reel in the sculpture have five spokes?

    a. Because there were only five awards in the beginning
    b. Because there were five people who produced the sculpture
    c. Because there used to be only five kinds of awards

5. Whose story about the Oscar name is the most popular?

    a. A writer's
    b. An actress'
    c. A librarian's

6. According to the reading, why did a newspaper writer give the trophy a person's name?

    a. Because he was a fan of Harmon Oscar Nelson
    b. Because he didn't like the Academy name
    c. Because he hoped the Academy Awards would give out more awards

7. Who is Harmon Oscar Nelson?

    a. The librarian's cousin
    b. The writer's uncle
    c. The actress' husband

T/F Questions

1. Currently, there are less than 24 Oscars given out at the Academy Awards. (**T** / **F**)

2. The official name of the Academy Awards is the Oscars. (**T** / **F**)

3. The number of Academy Awards given out has doubled since the first ceremony. (**T** / **F**)

Writing Questions

Make a full sentence, using the following words.

1. (attended / 300 / less / people / the / than / first) Academy Awards ceremony, which was held at the Roosevelt Hotel in Los Angeles.

   _____

2. In 1981, the Oscars were postponed for 24 hours (kill / because / tried / someone / President Ronald Reagan / to).

   _____

© Valeriya Zankovych / Shutterstock.com

Listening

Listen to the following "Reading 2." Fill in the correct word or phrase in each blank (a-e) and match the definitions below.

a. _____ b. _____ c. _____

d. _____ e. _____

1. complex
2. to ask someone to leave
3. immediate
4. comprises
5. cheer
6. complaint
7. declared

Reading 2 — Academy Members and Voting

1 The Academy of Motion Picture Arts and Sciences **(a)** about 8,000 film industry professionals. For the most part, the identity of these members is top secret. However, anyone who has ever been nominated for an Academy Award gets **(b)** admission into the association. In 2014, the Los
5 Angeles Times discovered that the membership was lacking in diversity, with most of the members being white and male. This caused a big **(c)**, and the Academy has since worked hard to give membership to more people of color, women, and people from countries outside of America.

2 Annually, these members are responsible for choosing the Academy
10 Award winners through a **(d)** voting process. First, members choose nominees from within their discipline. That is, only producers can nominate producers and only technicians can nominate technicians. However, everyone can vote for Best Picture. After this, the members vote again by choosing their favorite from a short list of nominees for
15 each award category. Finally, on the day of the Oscars, the winners are **(e)**.

NOTES
l. 5: **diversity** 多様性 l. 11: **discipline** 規律

Comprehension Questions

Choose the best answer (a-c).

1. How many people are members of the Academy of Motion Picture Arts and Sciences?
   - **a.** 2,014
   - **b.** 8,000
   - **c.** 18,000

2. What is NOT a way to become an Academy member?
   - **a.** By winning an Oscar
   - **b.** By becoming a nominee for an Academy Award
   - **c.** By being a film collector

3. Why did the Academy change their membership after 2014?
   - **a.** Because they had too many women members
   - **b.** Because too many of the members were from abroad
   - **c.** Because they needed to diversify

4. What happens every year at the Academy?
   - **a.** The Academy needs to report on their membership.
   - **b.** The Academy members need to vote for their favorite movie.
   - **c.** The Academy needs to reduce their membership.

5. Who would be able to nominate a producer for an award for Best Producer?
   - **a.** Someone who is a director
   - **b.** Anyone who is an active actor or actress
   - **c.** All producers who are Academy members

6. What is something that all Academy members CANNOT do?
   - **a.** They can nominate their favorite movie for an award.
   - **b.** They can nominate their favorite actor for an award.
   - **c.** They can receive a short list for voting for award winners.

7. What happens on the day of the Academy Awards?
   - **a.** The people with the most votes win Oscars.
   - **b.** The people nominated for awards receive Oscars.
   - **c.** The people who attend the Academy Awards vote for Oscar winners.

T/F Questions

1. All of the Academy members are known to the American people. (**T** / **F**)

2. The Los Angeles Times reported good news about the Academy. (**T** / **F**)

3. It could be said that before 2014, the Academy of Motion Picture Arts and Sciences was a club for white men. (**T** / **F**)

Writing Questions

Make a full sentence, using the following words.

1. In 2020, Joaquin Phoenix was given an Oscar for Best Performance by an Actor in a Leading Role (his / of / in / because / movie / acting / the) *Joker*.

   _____

2. (the / the / in / of / Academy Awards / history), three films hold the record of winning the most Academy Awards: *Ben-Hur*, *Titanic*, and *The Lord of the Rings: The Return of the King*.

   _____

© Sorbis / Shutterstock.com

Chapter 5

American Fashion

ファッション

> ニューヨーク市はパリ、ミラノ、ロンドンに並ぶ世界四大ファッション都市の一つです。1850年代は仕事着として、1930年代にはスポーツウェアとして人気になったジーンズのように、米国はファッション流行の発信地です。その米国で活躍するデザイナーについて読みましょう。

Reading 1 ▶ ## Warm-up

Using your dictionary, find the meanings of the following words.

1. mention	**2.** stand out	**3.** jockey	**4.** bully
5. preppy	**6.** loan	**7.** line	**8.** iconic

Choose the best answer (a-c).

1. What is the most famous fashion brand that started by selling only men's neckties?
   a. Tommy Hilfiger
   b. Polo
   c. Marc Jacobs

2. What does the word "logo" mean?
   a. ticket
   b. sticker
   c. symbol

1 America is home to numerous designer brands, and when people have discussions about the most famous fashion brands to come from America, the Ralph Lauren brand is always mentioned. In fact, the Ralph Lauren brand, born in 1967, is not only famous for the polo shirt and classic designs, but it is also famous for a logo that stands out from all other brands. It is the logo of the polo pony and jockey that was inspired by the gentleman's sport of polo.

2 Ralph Lifshitz was born in the Bronx, New York City, on October 14, 1939. In 1955, when he was 16 years old, Ralph and his brother changed their names to Lauren to escape the bullying they received because of their Jewish family name.

3 From a young age, Ralph Lauren had a sense for fashion. When he was in his teens, he was known for dressing in the preppy style of America's campus men who attended Ivy League universities. In fact, his fashion sense inspired him to get into the fashion business by designing his own brand of men's neckties called the Polo necktie in 1967. The ties were very popular, so the following year he got a loan and began designing a full line of menswear, which people loved. This gave Ralph the opportunity to become the first designer to open his own boutique in the luxury department store chain called Bloomingdales in 1970. In 1971, not only did Ralph open his first standalone store on Rodeo Drive in Beverly Hills, but he also released his brand of women's designer shirts and the company's iconic polo player logo. Following this, Ralph Lauren continued to successfully build his brand with each new design, making Polo one of the world's most recognizable American brands.

NOTES
l. 14: **Ivy League** 米国東海岸の州にある難関私立大学の総称。ブラウン大学、コロンビア大学、コーネル大学、ダートマス大学、ハーバード大学、ペンシルバニア大学、プリンストン大学、イェール大学の8大学がある。　l. 19: **opportunity** 機会　l. 21: **standalone store** 独立店舗

Comprehension Questions

Choose the best answer (a-c).

1. When was the Polo brand started?

   a. 1939

   b. 1967

   c. 1970

2. Why is the Polo logo so famous compared to other brands?

   a. Because it is a picture of a man on a horse playing a sport

   b. Because it is a picture of Ralph Lauren

   c. Because it debuted at Ivy League schools

3. How many people in Ralph's family have the Lauren name?

   a. One

   b. Two

   c. Four

4. Why did Ralph Lauren wear clothes similar to university men when he was younger?

   a. Because he thought their way of dressing was fashionable

   b. Because he wanted to get a job at an Ivy League school

   c. Because they wore the Polo logo that he loved

5. When did Ralph Lauren borrow money to make men's clothes?

   a. In 1967

   b. In 1968

   c. In 1971

6. What was unique about the boutique that Ralph opened in Bloomingdales?

   a. It was a shop that only had the Polo brand for sale.

   b. It sold both men's and women's clothes.

   c. It was where the Polo logo debuted.

7. Where was the first independent Polo clothing store started?

   a. In the Bronx, New York City

   b. In Beverly Hills

   c. In Bloomingdales

T/F Questions

Circle T or F for each of the following statements.

1. Ralph didn't like being called Lifshitz. (**T** / **F**)

2. The Polo logo began appearing on clothes in 1970. (**T** / **F**)

3. Ralph Lauren opened his first store the same year he designed women's shirts. (**T** / **F**)

Writing Questions

Make a full sentence, using the following words.

1. Ralph was the first designer (in / uniforms / for / who / history / made) Wimbledon.

   _____

2. In 1981, Ralph Lauren (store / opened / overseas / his / in / first) London, England.

   _____

© AVM Images / Shutterstock.com

Reading 2 ▶ Listening

🔊 Audio 11

Listen to the following "Reading 2." Fill in the correct word or phrase in each blank (a-e) and match the definitions below.

a. _____   b. _____   c. _____

d. _____   e. _____

1. invention
2. perfumes and colognes
3. to send someone away
4. to get someone to work for you
5. to say that someone has noticed something
6. unhappy
7. impressed

Reading 2 ◢ Tommy Hilfiger

The year was 1985, and America was about to be **(a)** with a new brand of clothing for men that would compete with some of the already famous American brands at the time, such as Ralph Lauren, Perry Ellis and Calvin Klein. This new brand, the **(b)** of Thomas Jacob "Tommy" Hilfiger, would soon become famous for its classic American cool style. In fact, the 5 hip-hop artist, Grand Puba, thought the brand was so cool that he mentioned the brand in one of his songs in 1992. This **(c)** inspired Tommy to actively promote his brand to the music community. As a result, in the 1990s, Tommy Hilfiger sponsored many artists' concert tours, such as Sheryl Crow, Britney Spears, and Lenny Kravitz, to name 10 a few. Also, Tommy **(d)** famous bands to play live at his fashion shows, which often lead to fashion models dancing on stage. Since 1985, the Tommy Hilfiger brand has expanded its product line to include women's and children's clothes, sportswear, shoes, accessories, watches, jewelry, and **(e)**. In addition, the brand is now sold in over 100 countries around 15 the world.

NOTES

l. 8: **promote** 宣伝する

Comprehension Questions

Choose the best answer (a-c).

1. What happened in 1985?

    a. A famous clothing company failed.

    b. A new brand of women's clothes was born.

    c. A fashion designer began selling clothes for men.

2. Why did Grand Puba sing about Tommy Hilfiger?

    a. Because he loved America's traditional fashion designers

    b. Because he wanted to have a child like Tommy

    c. Because he liked the brand's design

3. After hearing his brand mentioned in a song, what did Tommy Hilfiger do?

    a. He paid money to musicians to help advertise for him.

    b. He sold his company to another fashion company.

    c. He tried to become a hip-hop artist.

4. How did Tommy Hilfiger promote his brand to the music industry?

    a. He wrote songs for them.

    b. He funded some concert tours.

    c. He started his own band.

5. How many artist's concert tours did Tommy Hilfiger sponsor?

    a. Less than three

    b. Three

    c. More than three

6. What is something that did NOT happen at Tommy Hilfiger fashion shows?

    a. Models danced on stage

    b. Bands performed on stage

    c. Models gave modeling lessons

7. What kind of goods does Tommy Hilfiger NOT sell?

    a. Perfume

    b. Rings

    c. Cars

T/F Questions

Circle T or F for each of the following statements.

1. The Tommy Hilfiger brand was famous like Ralph Lauren in 1985. (**T** / **F**)

2. Tommy Hilfiger's real name is Thomas. (**T** / **F**)

3. In 1992, the Tommy Hilfiger brand got free advertising from a singer. (**T** / **F**)

Writing Questions

Make a full sentence, using the following words.

1. Tommy Hilfiger (that / is / built / a / famous / brand / for) its red, white, and blue label.

   _____

2. When Tommy (18, / opened / was / he / store / in / a) Elmira City that sold bell-bottoms, incense, and records.

   _____

Chapter 6

American Universities

アメリカの大学

> 米国で最も古く、世界で最も一流の大学として有名なハーバード大学は、1636年に創立し、1億8,000万冊以上の蔵書を誇る世界最大の図書館があります。そのハーバード大学にもある、米国の大学のクラブと学生生活について読んでみましょう。

Reading 1 ▶ **Warm-up**

Using your dictionary, find the meanings of the following words.

1. organization	**2.** similar	**3.** found	**4.** race
5. interracial	**6.** accept	**7.** vary	**8.** nevertheless

Choose the best answer (a-c).

1. What is something that American university students need to decide before starting school?

   a. Their Greek name

   b. Their race

   c. Whether to join a Greek organization

2. What does the word "divided" mean?

   a. created

   b. joined

   c. separated

Reading 1 — Fraternities and Sororities

🔊 Audio 12

1 After being accepted to an American university or college, new students will need to decide if they would like to join a fraternity or sorority. A fraternity is a social organization for male students, like a club, while a sorority is a similar organization for women.

A alpha	B beta	Γ gamma	Δ delta	E epsilon	Z zeta
H eta	Θ theta	I iota	K kappa	Λ lambda	M mu
N nu	Ξ xi	O omikron	Π pi	P rho	Σ sigma
T tau	Υ upsilon	Φ phi	X chi	Ψ psi	Ω omega

2 Fraternities and sororities are known as Greek organizations because the names of fraternities and sororities are based on the Greek alphabet. For example, Phi Beta Kappa is the name of the first American fraternity and was founded in 1776, while Kappa Alpha Theta, which began in 1870, is the name of the first sorority for women.

3 These brotherhoods and sisterhoods are typically joined because the members have similar interests and or religious backgrounds. In addition, these Greek organizations are known for their volunteer service and high academic achievement. However, fraternities and sororities have historically been divided by race. Alpha Phi Alpha, the first African American fraternity, became the first interracial fraternity by accepting its first non-black member in 1945, and Sigma Alpha Mu, a fraternity for Jews, started accepting non-Jewish members in 1953.

4 The cost of each Greek organization varies greatly. Some cost only a few hundred dollars per semester, while others cost several thousand dollars. Nevertheless, by choosing to "go Greek," students who attend an American university or college will find that when they arrive on campus, they gain a structured lifestyle and a strong support group. Also, after graduation, they will have many lifelong friends and professional connections that will help them advance their careers.

NOTES
l. 12: **Greek** ギリシャ語の　l. 24: **Jew** ユダヤ人、ユダヤ系の

Comprehension Questions

1. What is a fraternity?

    a. A club for female students

    b. An association for men

    c. A university name

2. When did the first sorority for women begin?

    a. 1776

    b. 1870

    c. 1953

3. What is NOT a reason to join a university brotherhood or sisterhood?

    a. Students want to be with people of the same sex.

    b. Students want to be with people of the same faith.

    c. Students want to join a coed club.

4. What is the name of the first African American fraternity?

    a. Alpha Phi Alpha

    b. Sigma Alpha Mu

    c. Phi Beta Kappa

5. When did Greek organizations start to become interracial?

    a. At the start of the 20th century

    b. During the middle of the 20th century

    c. Before the 1800s

6. What are fraternities and sororities famous for?

    a. Having members that have difficulty studying

    b. Having members who like to do community service

    c. Having members who do not like to socialize

7. How can students benefit from sororities and fraternities after graduation?

    a. They can take classes again to get the grade they want.

    b. They can find better jobs.

    c. They can make their own Greek association.

T/F Questions

Circle T or F for each of the following statements.

1. Students need to choose their sorority or fraternity when they apply to a university. (**T** / **F**)

2. Some sororities and fraternities are very cheap. (**T** / **F**)

3. A woman who joins a sorority will likely have difficulty finding help with her studies. (**T** / **F**)

Writing Questions

Make a full sentence, using the following words.

1. "Going Greek" is a good way (quickly / many / students / for / friends / to make).

   _____

2. The first American fraternity (students / that / made / could / so / was) discuss serious matters in private.

   _____

Listening

🔊 Audio 13

Listen to the following "Reading 2." Fill in the correct word or phrase in each blank (a-e) and match the definitions below.

a. _____   b. _____   c. _____

d. _____   e. _____

1. stay at
2. optional subject
3. four-year
4. reject
5. move
6. fit
7. core curriculum

Reading 2 ▸ **Higher Education in America**

After graduating from high school in the US, students who choose to study at a college or university will choose to study for a **(a)** degree. A bachelor's degree is also called an undergraduate degree. Typically, the first two years of school consist of **(b)** that are common to all students.

5 During these two years, freshmen, first-year students, and sophomores, second-year students, take courses such as math, history, literature, and communications, so that they can broaden their knowledge in as many subjects as possible. However, in years three and four, when students are juniors and seniors, they will focus on their major by choosing **(c)**

10 that **(d)** their interests and strengths. In America, it is not necessary for students to stay at the same university for four years. In fact, it is quite common for students to apply to **(e)** to a better university after one or two years of undergraduate study. In fact, Steven Spielberg, George Lucas, and Barack Obama are examples of some famous people who

15 have transferred universities.

NOTES
l. 3: **bachelor's degree** 学士号　l. 7: **broaden one's knowledge** 知識の幅をひろげる　l. 15: **transfer** 編入する

Comprehension Questions

Choose the best answer (a-c).

1. What can students do after they graduate from high school?

    a. Skip their first two years of university

    b. Go to a college or university

    c. Transfer to a different university

2. What do students who enter university study for after leaving high school?

    a. An undergraduate degree

    b. A graduate degree

    c. An elective degree

3. What do students usually study during years one and two at university?

    a. The courses that they are most interested in

    b. The courses that focus on their major

    c. The courses that give them broad knowledge

4. What is NOT an example of a required course?

    a. Literature

    b. Advanced writing

    c. History

5. What is another name for a second-year student?

    a. Sophomore

    b. Junior

    c. Freshman

6. Why do students take elective courses in their third and fourth years of university?

    a. Because they want to learn about as many different things as possible

    b. Because they really like their core curriculum

    c. Because they want to study subjects that they like

7. Who would typically want to go to a different university after one or two years of study in America?

    a. Someone who is satisfied with the quality of his or her education

    b. Someone who hopes to graduate from a more prestigious school

    c. Someone who likes their university's elective courses

T/F Questions

Circle T or F for each of the following statements.

1. A senior will typically finish his or her bachelor's degree within one year. (**T** / **F**)

2. American university students cannot choose their electives. (**T** / **F**)

3. George Lucas is a famous person who changed his university. (**T** / **F**)

Writing Questions

Make a full sentence, using the following words.

1. (said / it / been / has / former / that) President Barack Obama may be the world's most famous transfer student.

   _____

2. My parents want me (a / to / to / more / transfer / and / bigger) academic university next year.

   _____

© REDPIXEL.PL / Shutterstock.com

Chapter 7

American Social Networking

ソーシャルネットワーキング

> ソーシャルメディアとソーシャルネットワーキングは同じだと思っていませんか？　前者は人からまたは人へ情報を送受信する場である一方、後者は仕事や学校、娯楽のために人とのつながりを可能にする技術です。米国にはどのようなものがあるか読んでみましょう。

Reading 1 **Warm-up**

Using your dictionary, find the meanings of the following words.

1. phenomenon	**2.** networking	**3.** provide	**4.** viral
5. fast forward	**6.** countless	**7.** attraction	**8.** interact

Choose the best answer (a-c).

1. What does the word "network" mean?

   a. meet

   b. avoid

   c. part

2. What is something that dramatically changed American society in the 1990s?

   a. Politics

   b. Sports

   c. SNS

Reading 1　Twitter

1 In 1997, America gave birth to a phenomenon that would forever change the world. The phenomenon is called social media, and in 1997, SixDegrees.com became the first of many companies to provide a social networking service (SNS) for users. SixDegrees.com allowed people to
5　network with friends in a way that is similar to Facebook. That is, people would sign up with their email address, make a profile, and then add friends to their network. Fast forward to today, and you will discover that not only is over 70% of the American population using at least one kind of social media, but there are countless social media sites and more
10　than 2.6 billion social media users around the world. In fact, social media sites like Facebook, Instagram, and YouTube have over a billion monthly active users.

2 Twitter is one of the many internet sites that was born during the social media boom that occurred at the beginning of the 21st century.
15　Twitter isn't as popular as many other social media sites, but its 335 million regular users like using it because it provides them with real-time information, similar to live TV news. The big difference between Twitter and Facebook is that Twitter is public by default. This means that when a user tweets or posts something, their news can be spread to
20　many people around the world very quickly. In fact, when a tweet becomes very popular, it is seen as going viral. Another attraction that Twitter has for people is that users can interact with their friends and celebrities alike. Also, Twitter users like this social media site because they get to be like reporters, and when their tweet goes viral, they can
25　enjoy a bit of fame, like the celebrities they follow.

NOTES
l. 14: **boom** 急成長　l. 18: **by default** 初期設定で　l. 25: **a bit of** ちょっとした

Comprehension Questions

Choose the best answer (a-c).

1. What happened in America in 1997?

   a. The American population became more than one billion.

   b. Facebook was launched.

   c. SixDegrees.com started the SNS boom.

2. Which is something that is NOT common between Facebook and SixDegrees. com?

   a. They both require internet service to use.

   b. They started at the same time.

   c. Their users post their personal profiles online.

3. According to the reading, what kind of person would enjoy using an SNS?

   a. Someone who likes keeping in touch with friends

   b. Someone who was born before the 20th century

   c. Someone who doesn't like to connect with people

4. How many people use social media in the world today?

   a. Almost 70 million people

   b. Nearly one billion people

   c. More than two billion people

5. When did social media experience the most growth in popularity?

   a. Around 1997

   b. During the 2000s

   c. Within the last 10 years

6. What makes Twitter so unique compared to Facebook?

   a. Users can share information with people in different countries.

   b. Twitter has more followers than Facebook.

   c. Posts by Twitter users are always private.

7. Why would people use Twitter instead of Facebook?

   a. Because they hope to become a famous movie star

   b. Because they want to act like a reporter

   c. Because they desire to see a celebrity's new movie

T/F Questions

Circle T or F for each of the following statements.

1. Facebook has more than 335 million active monthly users. (**T** / **F**)

2. News that becomes popular very quickly is viral news. (**T** / **F**)

3. It is easier to become famous with Facebook than Twitter (**T** / **F**)

Writing Questions

Make a full sentence, using the following words.

1. (is / a / limit / there / tweets / 140-character / for) in Chinese, Japanese, and Korean.

   _____

2. Mark Zuckerberg and some of his (Facebook / friends / made / as / SNS / an) for Harvard University students.

   _____

Reading 2 **Listening**

🔊 Audio 15

Listen to the following "Reading 2." Fill in the correct word or phrase in each blank (a-e) and match the definitions below.

a. _____ b. _____ c. _____

d. _____ e. _____

1. additionally
2. closed
3. digital content
4. give away
5. at first
6. began
7. therefore

Reading 2 · Minds—Getting Paid for Posting

Minds, **(a)** in 2015, could become the new standard for how social networking services should operate. **(b)**, the app looks similar to other SNS apps. However, Minds operates much differently. For example, Minds doesn't sell users' information to companies so that companies can advertise to the users who would most likely buy their product. Also, 5 users will see posts in their **(c)** in reverse-chronological order; the older, unread posts will appear first. In addition, Minds is open source. That is, people can access the programming code for the app to help improve it. **(d)**, Minds offers users a chance to get paid for creating content, posting, and sharing information. So, how does this work? If a user posts 10 something or spends time using the app, the user will get paid a kind of money called a "token." The more popular the post or the more the app is used, the more tokens a user can get. These tokens can then be used to promote or receive content, like paying for advertising, buy content that the user likes or be **(e)** to other users. 15

NOTES
l. 6: **reverse-** 逆の、反対の　l. 6: **chronological** 年代順の

Comprehension Questions

1. When could people start to use the Minds app?

   a. Before 2015

   b. From 2015

   c. After 2050

2. What does the speaker think about SNS companies?

   a. They should be like Minds.

   b. They should have started in 2015.

   c. They should get paid tokens.

3. What does Minds do to users' information?

   a. They sell it to advertising companies.

   b. The give it to other users.

   c. They keep it from companies who would like to buy it.

4. What is unique about the posts in a user's Minds feed?

   a. They have many advertisements.

   b. The newest posts are at the bottom.

   c. Older posts are seen last.

5. What can people do to the programing of the Minds app?

   a. They can edit it.

   b. They can sell it.

   c. They can buy it.

6. What can Minds users get for making a comment about another user's post?

   a. They can get products from companies.

   b. They can get open source information.

   c. They can get something like money.

7. What is something that CANNOT be done with Minds tokens?

   a. They can be traded with other users.

   b. They can be used to promote content.

   c. They can be given to other people who use the Minds app.

T/F Questions

Circle T or F for each of the following statements.

1. Because Minds is open source software, it cannot be altered. (**T** / **F**)

2. The more posts Minds users make, the more tokens they can get. (**T** / **F**)

3. Tokens can be borrowed from other Minds users. (**T** / **F**)

Writing Questions

Make a full sentence, using the following words.

1. (about / active / monthly / 110,000 / with / users), Minds is a relatively small SNS company.

   _____

2. In the future, Minds (to / able / users / be / may / exchange) their tokens into dollars or a cryptocurrency.

   _____

© Grzegorz Czapski / Shutterstock.com

American Innovators and Innovation

アメリカの革新者と新技術

" 2018 年に米国の造幣局が偉大な発明をした 56 人を選ぶ「アメリカン・イノベーション 1 ドル硬貨プログラム」を始め、コロンビア特別区、50 州の各地域などから発明者や技術革新者を称えて、2032 年まで毎年 4 枚新硬貨を発行します。今後誰がどのような技術を生み出すのでしょうか? "

Reading 1 **Warm-up**

Using your dictionary, find the meanings of the following words.

1. founding   **2.** innovator   **3.** invention   **4.** revolutionize

5. as a whole   **6.** fulfill   **7.** affordable   **8.** discover

Choose the best answer (a-c).

1. Which American inventor started PayPal?

   a. Elon Musk

   b. Benjamin Franklin

   c. Thomas Edison

2. What does the phrase "household name" mean?

   a. famous

   b. unknown

   c. appliance

🔊 Audio 16

1 Ever since the founding of America in 1776, American innovators have been making inventions that have revolutionized America and the world. Some, like Thomas Edison who invented the first commercially viable light bulb and phonograph, are well known, while others, like Steven Sasson who invented the digital camera, are less famous. 5 Currently, there is Elon Musk, an innovator who is already a household name in America for his Tesla electric car and SolarCity. However, it will not be long before he becomes famous all over the world, thanks to the increasing popularity of PayPal and SpaceX. In fact, not only has *Forbes* called Musk one of America's most innovative leaders, but CNBC 10 has said that Musk could be the Thomas Edison of today.

2 According to people who have worked with Musk, what makes him such a powerful innovator is the fact that he has the ability to sense what people will want or need in the future. Moreover, Musk, like many other great innovators, including Edison, is skilled at studying problems 15 with Aristotle's first-principles technique. That is, to solve a problem, you don't look at the problem as a whole, but instead, you look at all of the parts that make up the problem. Musk used this principle when trying to fulfill his dream of creating a future society where everyone drives electric cars. The problem that needed to be solved was how to 20 make electric cars affordable, and that meant creating cars with cheaper batteries. To make a cheaper battery, Musk examined all of the parts that were used to make a battery, and when he did this, he discovered that he could buy all the parts of a battery and build it himself, which allowed him to make a cheaper battery and car. 25

NOTES　l. 4: **viable** 実行可能な、発展しうる　l. 10: **CNBC** Consumer News and Business Channel の略。米国ニュージャージー州に本社のあるニュース専門局。　l. 16: **Aristotle** アリストテレス (B.C. 384-322)、古代ギリシャの哲学者。

Comprehension Questions

Choose the best answer (a-c).

1. How long has the United States been a country?

   a. More than 300 years

   b. Since the birth of Thomas Edison

   c. About 250 years

2. According to the reading, which kinds of people have made major changes to American society?

   a. People who look like Thomas Edison

   b. People who make new things

   c. People who build electric cars

3. What did Steve Sasson invent?

   a. The first digital camera

   b. The first record player

   c. The first electric light bulb

4. In the future, Elon Musk will become more famous in other countries because…

   a. he is planning to build a new kind of electric car.

   b. his inventions will become more popular.

   c. he makes high quality household electronics.

5. Why is Musk such a powerful innovator?

   a. Because he understands what technology will be popular in the future

   b. Because he knows what people want today

   c. Because he has worked with many famous people

6. What skill is common to Musk and other famous inventors?

   a. The ability to fix things by looking at the problem as a whole.

   b. The ability to make things cheaper.

   c. The ability to solve problems like by using Aristotle's advice.

7. What did Musk do to discover how to make cheaper electric cars?

   a. He had a meeting with Aristotle.

   b. He used the first-principles technique.

   c. He found a company to make cheaper batteries.

T/F Questions

Circle T or F for each of the following statements.

1. Musk dreamed of a society where no one drove in gas powered cars. (**T** / **F**)

2. Most electric cars are expensive because of the cost of the battery. (**T** / **F**)

3. Elon Musk is as good of an innovator as Thomas Edison. (**T** / **F**)

Writing Questions

Make a full sentence, using the following words.

1. When Musk was a child, he would (about / that / so / daydream / inventions / much) his parents thought he had a hearing problem.

   _____

2. Musk went to Stanford University for a Ph.D. in energy physics, but dropped out after two days (to / because / make / wanted / an Internet company / he).

   _____

© IrinaK / Shutterstock.com

Listen to the following "Reading 2." Fill in the correct word or phrase in each blank (a-e) and match the definitions below.

a. _____ b. _____ c. _____

d. _____ e. _____

1. limited
2. achieve
3. several
4. populate
5. miss
6. an important accomplishment
7. a path around the earth

Reading 2 SpaceX

In 2002, Elon Musk founded his third company because he wanted to **(a)** his dream of helping people to live on other planets. More specifically, it is his goal to make space travel affordable so that people can **(b)** Mars. To help him realize this dream, he created the Space Exploration
5 Technologies Corporation, more commonly known as SpaceX. Since its founding, this company has already reached a number of important **(c)**. Firstly, it has developed the world's first reusable rocket. Also, SpaceX rockets have launched satellites into space, including one in a low, geostationary **(d)** and another in a high L1 orbit, and is currently
10 working on putting 12,000 Starlink satellites into orbit, 60 at a time, so that everyone in the world no matter where they live can have access to cheap and reliable high-speed internet. Lastly, SpaceX has made **(e)** flights carrying astronauts and supplies for NASA to and from the International Space Station and has developed Starship, the rocket that
15 is going to be used to fly people to the moon by 2023 and Mars by 2024.

NOTES   l. 7: **reusable** 再利用できる   l. 8: **satellite** 人工衛星   l. 9: **geostationary** 〔衛星が〕静止した   l. 10: **orbit** 軌道   l. 13: **astronaut** 宇宙飛行士   l. 13: **NASA** National Aeronautics and Space Administration、アメリカ航空宇宙局

Comprehension Questions

1. What is the name of Elon Musk's third company?

   a. Starlink

   b. SpaceX

   c. NASA

2. What date represents the start of the Space Exploration Technologies Corporation?

   a. 2002

   b. 2023

   c. 2024

3. What is Musk's dream?

   a. To see people living on Mars

   b. To pilot a rocket

   c. To live on Starship

4. What has SpaceX done that no other company has done?

   a. It made a rocket that can be used many times.

   b. Its rockets can fly around the world 60 times each flight.

   c. It is the first company to colonize Mars.

5. What is NOT true about SpaceX rockets?

   a. They put many satellites around the earth.

   b. They can carry 60 satellites.

   c. They have been to Mars.

6. Why do SpaceX rockets fly to the International Space Station?

   a. Because people want to vacation there

   b. Because NASA astronauts need to go there

   c. Because it is in need of internet service

7. How many Starlink satellites are going to be used to create high-speed internet service for the future?

   a. 60

   b. 2,012

   c. 12,000

Chapter 8: American Innovators and Innovation

T/F Questions

1. An L1 orbit is high above the earth. (**T** / **F**)

2. There have been many trips by SpaceX to the International Space Station. (**T** / **F**)

3. SpaceX will fly people to Mars by 2023 and the moon 2024. (**T** / **F**)

Writing Questions

Make a full sentence, using the following words.

1. Last Saturday, SpaceX launched a Falcon 9 rocket with (carrying / two / Crew Dragon capsule / NASA / the / astronauts).

   _____

2. The Crew Dragon capsule uses solar panels (power / to generate / the / for / re-entry / spacecraft's) to Earth's atmosphere.

   _____

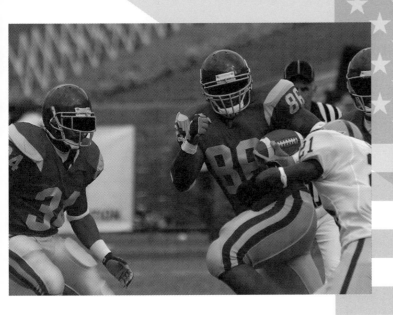

Chapter 9

American Football

アメリカンフットボール

> アメフトの最高の大会であるスーパーボールのハーフタイムの演奏は、昔は高校や大学の吹奏楽団が演奏していました。1993年にテレビの視聴率を上げるため、有名なアーティストを起用し始めましたが、起用された最初の人物はマイケル・ジャクソンでした。

Reading 1 Warm-up

Using your dictionary, find the meanings of the following words.

1. origin
2. rivalry
3. spectator
4. merge
5. inaugural
6. compete
7. temporarily
8. moniker

Choose the best answer (a-c).

1. What is the biggest sporting event for Americans?

   a. The World Series
   b. The Super Bowl
   c. The NBA Championship

2. What does the phrase "sporting event" mean?

   a. a meeting
   b. a fight
   c. a competition

🔊 Audio 18

1 The National Football League (NFL) championship game, better known as the Super Bowl, is not as old as other great sporting events, like the World Series of Major League Baseball (MLB), but it has become an important event for most Americans.

5   **2** The origin of the Super Bowl began in 1960 with the American Football League (AFL). A group of businessmen wanted to start a new league to compete against the NFL because they were frustrated that the NFL did not want to expand the number of teams. The rivalry between the NFL and AFL over the next decade helped make American

10 football the most popular spectator sport in the country.

3 By 1966, an agreement was made between NFL Commissioner, Pete Rozelle, and Lamar Hunt, owner of the AFL's Kansas City Chiefs, to merge the two leagues by 1970. In the meantime, the champions of each league would compete against each other at the end of the season. Hunt

15 temporarily suggested calling this new championship game the "Super Bowl," and the moniker stuck as sportswriters had already begun using the name before the inaugural game in 1967. In this game, nearly 65 million viewers watched the NFL's Green Bay Packers win the Super Bowl in Los Angeles, making it the largest sporting event in America at

20 the time.

4 After the two leagues merged in 1970, the NFL created the American Football Conference (AFC) and the National Football Conference (NFC), and at the end of each season the winning teams from each conference play each other in the Super Bowl.

NOTES
l. 7: **be frustrated** 挫折する   l. 9: **decade** 10 年   l. 13: **in the meantime** その間にも、それまで

Comprehension Questions

Choose the best answer (a-c).

1. What year was the first Super Bowl held?

    a. In 1966

    b. In 1967

    c. In 1970

2. Who wanted to create the AFL to compete with the NFL?

    a. Pete Rozelle

    b. The fans of American football

    c. A group of businessmen

3. Why was the AFL created?

    a. Because fans wanted more American football games

    b. Because the NFL did not have good players

    c. Because the NFL had a limited number of teams

4. How many conferences are there in the new NFL?

    a. One

    b. Two

    c. Three

5. Where was the first Super Bowl held?

    a. In Kansas City

    b. In Green Bay

    c. In Los Angeles

6. When did the NFL and the AFL officially join together?

    a. In 1966

    b. In 1967

    c. In 1970

7. Who won the first Super Bowl?

    a. The Kansas City Chiefs

    b. The Los Angeles Rams

    c. The Green Bay Packers

T/F Questions

Circle T or F for each of the following statements.

1. The Super Bowl is older than the World Series. (**T** / **F**)

2. The first Super Bowl was watched by almost 65 million people. (**T** / **F**)

3. Lamar Hunt, owner of the AFL's Kansas City Chiefs, suggested the name, Super Bowl. (**T** / **F**)

Writing Questions

Make a full sentence, using the following words.

1. The origin of the Super Bowl (as / with / back / began / far / as / 1960) the American Football League (AFL).

   _____

2. By 1966, (an / made / Pete Rozelle / was / agreement / NFL Commissioner / between) and Lamar Hunt.

   _____

© hkalkan / Shutterstock.com

Reading 2 ▶ Listening

Audio 19

Listen to the following "Reading 2." Fill in the correct word or phrase in each blank (a-e) and match the definitions below.

a. _____ **b.** _____ **c.** _____

d. _____ **e.** _____

1. to ban or disallow

2. to be honest or genuine

3. as a result

4. to object or oppose something

5. to take a position

6. to commit to something

7. to extend or elevate

Reading 2 — Colin Kaepernick

1 During the 2016 NFL season, Colin Kaepernick, the quarterback for the San Francisco 49ers, took a knee during the singing of the national anthem. This was his way of **(a)** social and racial injustices in the United States, and as a result, led to him leaving his team and, unfortunately, the NFL. 5

2 At that time, the NFL struggled with how to deal with the publicity the protests raised on current injustices. Instead of listening to and supporting its players, new rules, including fines for teams and players like Kaepernick, were introduced to **(b)** protesting during the national anthem. However, the NFL has only recently changed its **(c)** in 2020 by 10 acknowledging its mistakes and is now making efforts to be a part of positive change.

3 Following the death of George Floyd and the **(d)** Black Lives Matter protests across the nation, the NFL has shown rare unity with players, coaches, owners, and league officials publicly supporting for more to be 15 done against racial and social injustices. For instance, the NFL has already promised up to $250 million over the next ten years to support new social programs.

4 However, for the NFL's new position to feel **(e)**, the NFL must address
20 Colin Kaepernick. Many players acknowledge the importance of his
original decision to protest and feel he deserves an apology and a chance
to play again in the NFL.

NOTES
l. 2: **take a knee** 片ひざをつく　ll. 2-3: **national anthem** 国歌　l. 8: **fine** 罰金

Comprehension Questions

Choose the best answer (a-c).

1. What was Kaepernick protesting when he took a knee?

   a. The team's poor play

   b. The positive things happening in the United States

   c. The negative things happening in society

2. When was the last time Kaepernick played in the NFL?

   a. In 2016

   b. In 2018

   c. In 2020

3. How did the NFL react to the protests Kaepernick started?

   a. They supported him and other players.

   b. They tried to stop players from protesting.

   c. They created new rules to help the players.

4. What did the NFL do in 2020?

   a. Tried to be part of the positive changes in society

   b. Hired more players to protest

   c. Fined players money who tried to protest

5. What has had the biggest impact on people, companies, and organizations like
   the NFL in 2020?

   a. High unemployment

   b. The Black Lives Matter movement

   c. The presidential election

6. How much money has the NFL promised towards social programs?

   a. $250,000

   b. $25,000,000

   c. $250,000,000

7. How do current and former players feel about Kaepernick?

   a. They believe he tried to do the right thing, but the NFL didn't support him.

   b. They believe he is a great football player.

   c. They believe he needs to apologize to the NFL.

T/F Questions

Circle T or F for each of the following statements.

1. Colin Kaepernick played for the NFL's San Francisco Broncos. (**T** / **F**)

2. The NFL has admitted to making mistakes regarding previous player protests. (**T** / **F**)

3. Players think Kaepernick should get another chance to play in the NFL. (**T** / **F**)

Writing Questions

Make a full sentence, using the following words.

1. Many players (his / acknowledge / importance / the / of) original decision to protest.

   _____

2. (of / the / following / George Floyd / death) and the ensuing Black Lives Matter protests across the nation, American society is at a crossroads.

   _____

© Sean Pavone / Shutterstock.com

Chapter 10

Hollywood

ハリウッド

tinsel

> ロサンゼルスは米国でティンセルタウン（Tinseltown）と呼ばれているのを知っていますか？ ハリウッドの映画産業がクリスマスツリーに飾るティンセルのように、ピカピカの街にしてしまったところからこの名前がついたそうです。

Reading 1 ▶ **Warm-up**

Using your dictionary, find the meanings of the following words.

1. glitz **2.** humble **3.** upscale **4.** industry
5. ideal **6.** picturesque **7.** backdrop **8.** icon

Choose the best answer (a-c).

1. What do tourists want to do the most when they come to Los Angeles, U.S.A.?

a. Go to the beaches

b. Go shopping

c. Visit Hollywood

2. What does the phrase "cultural heritage" mean?

a. To have historical importance

b. To have long culture

c. To have many different cultures

Reading 1   Humble Beginnings

🔊 Audio 20

1 Hollywood, located in Los Angeles, California is known for its glitz and celebrities as the show-business capital of the world. However, Hollywood has humble beginnings as a small community.

2 In 1887, Hollywood only had one main street, Prospect Avenue, a post office, a hotel, and some upscale homes. Later, in 1902, H. J. Whitley, 5 better known as the "Father of Hollywood" helped the town grow and expand until it merged with Los Angeles in 1910. Whitley's efforts included opening the Hollywood Hotel on Prospect Avenue, which was changed to the now-famous Hollywood Boulevard. Today, the hotel is named the Dolby Theater, the place where the Oscars ceremony is held 10 every year.

3 Hollywood is also known for its movies. By 1911, the origins of the motion-picture industry began in Hollywood with the first movie studio on Sunset Boulevard, another famous street. By 1915, many major film companies had moved to Hollywood. One of the main reasons was that 15 Hollywood was ideal for making movies. California's warm and sunny weather and picturesque landscapes made for perfect backdrops for many movies.

4 Another important piece of Hollywood's history and a cultural icon is its famous tourist attraction, the Hollywood Sign. The sign, which is 20 located in the Hollywood Hills, was first built in 1923, and it originally said, "Hollywoodland." Each letter was 30 feet wide and 43 feet tall and the entire sign was lit up with 4,000 light bulbs. The Hollywood sign was later restored in 1949, but the last four letters were removed.

NOTES
l. 20: **tourist attraction** 観光名所   l. 24: **restore** 再建する、復元させる

Comprehension Questions

1. What did Hollywood NOT have in its small community in 1887?

   a. A school

   b. A hotel

   c. A post office

2. Who was known as the "Father of Hollywood"?

   a. Harry Chandler

   b. H. J. Whitley

   c. Harvey H. Wilcox

3. What year did Hollywood merge with Los Angeles?

   a. In 1902

   b. In 1910

   c. In 1911

4. Which famous street was the Hollywood Hotel located on?

   a. Hollywood Boulevard

   b. Sunset Boulevard

   c. Dolby Boulevard

5. When did the first movie studio come to Hollywood?

   a. In 1910

   b. In 1911

   c. In 1915

6. Why did the movie studios come to Hollywood?

   a. Because many celebrities lived there

   b. Because it was easy to make movies there

   c. Because of the beautiful scenery and nice weather

7. How big are the letters of the Hollywood Sign?

   a. 30 feet wide and 43 feet tall

   b. 43 feet wide and 30 feet tall

   c. 40 feet wide and 34 feet tall

T/F Questions

Circle T or F for each of the following statements.

1. The Oscars ceremony is held every year at the Hollywood Theater. (**T** / **F**)

2. The first movie studio in Hollywood was on Sunset Boulevard. (**T** / **F**)

3. The original Hollywood Sign was named "Hollywoodland." (**T** / **F**)

Writing Questions

Make a full sentence, using the following words.

1. The sign, (located / is / which / Hollywood Hills / in / the), was first built in 1923.

_____

2. The Hollywood Sign was not expected to last very long (become / the / nor / famous landmark / that) it is.

_____

© pablopicasso / Shutterstock.com

Listen to the following "Reading 2." Fill in the correct word or phrase in each blank (a-e) and match the definitions below.

a. _____ b. _____ c. _____

d. _____ e. _____

1. a group of businesses that make a kind of goods or services
2. to be accepted
3. a person who visits a place by choice and interest
4. the process of thinking about activities to achieve a goal
5. to keep
6. the top surface of a room
7. to consist of

Reading 2 — The Hollywood Walk of Fame

1 The Hollywood Walk of Fame is world famous and around 10 million tourists visit it every year. It is 15 blocks long and is **(a)** more than 2,600 bronze and stone stars placed in the sidewalk with most along Hollywood Boulevard. Each star costs about $30,000 and has a famous person's
5 name on it. However, how the idea for the stars began is unclear, but some guess it came from the historic Hollywood Hotel which had stars on its **(b)** with names of celebrities painted on them.

2 Businessman E. M. Stuart began planning the Walk of Fame in 1953 as a way to **(c)** the historic area's glitzy status. However, the first star
10 was not placed until 1960 for movie producer Stanley Kramer. Today, a star is awarded to anyone from the five **(d)** categories of film, television, radio, music, and theater, and anyone can have more than one star. Gene Autry is the only celebrity to have a star in each category. Finally, the most stars on the Walk of Fame have been awarded to the film **(e)**.

NOTES l. 2: **block**〔2 組の平行な道路で区切られた〕街区の短いほうを指す。正式な定義はないものの一般には 20 ブロック＝ 1 マイル（約 1.6km）とし、1 ブロックは約 80m に相当する。 l. 9: **glitzy** 派手な

Comprehension Questions

Choose the best answer (a-c).

1. How many people visit the Walk of Fame each year?

    a. 1 million

    b. 10 million

    c. 100,000 thousand

2. Where can you find the Walk of Fame?

    a. On Hollywood Boulevard

    b. On Sunset Boulevard

    c. On Theater Boulevard

3. How much does each star on the Walk of Fame cost?

    a. $3,000

    b. $30,000

    c. $40,000

4. What is each star on the Walk of Fame made of?

    a. Stone

    b. Bronze and stone

    c. Brass and stone

5. When was the first star placed in the Walk of Fame?

    a. In 1949

    b. In 1953

    c. In 1960

6. Why was the Walk of Fame created?

    a. Because it made money for businesses

    b. Because businessmen wanted to keep Hollywood's famous image

    c. Because it would bring a lot of tourists to Hollywood

7. Which of the following is NOT one of the five recognized categories for receiving a star?

    a. Theater

    b. Music

    c. News media

T/F Questions

Circle T or F for each of the following statements.

1. There are more than 2,600 stars on the Walk of Fame. (**T** / **F**)

2. Gene Autry is the first person to have a star on the Walk of Fame. (**T** / **F**)

3. It is not clear where the original idea for the Walk of Fame came from. (**T** / **F**)

Writing Questions

Make a full sentence, using the following words.

1. Gene Autry is the only celebrity (have / star / to / each / a / in / category).

   _____

2. Finally, the most stars on (the / have / to / been / Walk of Fame / awarded) the film industry.

   _____

© Ritu Manoj Jethani / Shutterstock.com

Chapter 11

Walt Disney

ウォルト・ディズニー

> ウォルト・ディズニーは 20 歳のとき、自身のキャリアの出発点である「ラフォグラム社」を立ち上げました。生涯にわたり数多くの作品を世に出しましたが、最も有名なキャラクターであるミッキーマウスはどのようにして生まれたか知っていますか？

Reading 1 ▶ ## Warm-up

Using your dictionary, find the meanings of the following words.

1. distribute   2. rave   3. animator   4. personality

5. laurel   6. theme   7. feature   8. debut

Choose the best answer (a-c).

1. Where do you think Walt Disney made his name in show business?

   a. In Florida

   b. In Kansas City

   c. In Hollywood

2. What does the phrase "to be a visionary" mean?

   a. To be able to see well

   b. To have great power

   c. To think about the future

Reading 1 — The Man Behind the Mouse

🔊 Audio 22

1 In the summer of 1923, Walt Disney, a young and talented artist, left Kansas City to come to California to be closer to his brother Roy. Soon after, he successfully sold his first short film called *Alice's Wonderland* and signed a contract to produce a series called *Alice Comedies*, which
5 would be distributed by M. J. Winkler from New York. To produce the series, Walt and Roy started Disney Brothers Cartoon Studio, which was soon renamed to the now-famous Walt Disney Studios.

2 After four years of successfully producing *Alice Comedies*, Walt Disney released a new cartoon in 1928, the first with sound, called
10 *Steamboat Willie*. It opened to rave reviews and the world was introduced to Mickey Mouse. Interestingly, Walt and his chief animator, Ub Iwerks, originally named their character Mortimer Mouse, but quickly thought Mickey was a better moniker to use. By giving Mickey personality, with Walt being the voice of Mickey, the famous mouse
15 became immediately popular.

3 Walt did not rest on his laurels and continued to create new cartoons along with his Mickey series. The new cartoons expanded to include new characters and stories based on emotional and musical themes. This led to the first full-color cartoon, *Flowers and Trees*, which won the very first
20 Academy Award for Best Cartoon in 1932. Walt Disney and his studio went on to win 22 Oscars, which is the current record.

4 In 1934, Walt Disney, the visionary, decided to make his first feature film. It took three years to make, but when *Snow White and the Seven Dwarfs* debuted in 1937, it was a hit. Walt Disney knew from then on
25 that the future would be in making animated films.

NOTES
l. 12: **Mortimer Mouse** Mortimer はのちに別のキャラクターとしてディズニーの作品に登場している。

Comprehension Questions

Choose the best answer (a-c).

1. When did Walt Disney move to California?

   a. In 1923

   b. In 1928

   c. In 1937

2. How long did Walt Disney make the Alice Comedies series?

   a. 2 years

   b. 3 years

   c. 4 years

3. Which cartoon introduced Mickey Mouse to the world?

   a. *Alice's Wonderland*

   b. *Alice Comedies*

   c. *Steamboat Willie*

4. Why was Mickey Mouse immediately popular with fans?

   a. Because he was the cutest character at the time

   b. Because he had a personality

   c. Because no other characters looked like him

5. By 1932, what made Walt Disney's new cartoons different from his previous ones?

   a. They were the first ones with sound.

   b. They made him more money.

   c. They introduced stories with different themes.

6. How many Academy Awards has Walt Disney won?

   a. 22

   b. 23

   c. 32

7. What is the name of Walt Disney's very first animated feature film?

   a. *Flowers and Trees*

   b. *Snow White and the Seven Dwarfs*

   c. *Steamboat Willie*

T/F Questions

Circle T or F for each of the following statements.

1. Walt Disney Studios was the original name of Walt and Roy's company. (**T** / **F**)

2. Animator Ub Iwerks helped Walt Disney design Mickey Mouse. (**T** / **F**)

3. Walt Disney was the original voice of Mickey Mouse. (**T** / **F**)

Writing Questions

Make a full sentence, using the following words.

1. Walt did not rest on his laurels (and / to / new / continued / cartoons / create) along with his Mickey series.

   _____

2. Walt Disney knew from then on, (future / be / making / in / that / the / would) animated films.

   _____

© Ferreiro / Shutterstock.com

Reading 2 **Listening**

 Audio 23

Listen to the following "Reading 2." Fill in the correct word or phrase in each blank (a-e) and match the definitions below.

a. _____ b. _____ c. _____

d. _____ e. _____

1. to expand
2. to be fake, not real
3. something very special
4. beyond a reasonable, safe, or permissible limit
5. to have a strong, special interest in something
6. something beautiful or delightful that is not from everyday life
7. a condition of being liked or supported by many people

Reading 2   **Imagining Disneyland**

1 After success in movies and television, Walt Disney wanted to **(a)** into amusement parks because he felt there was not an amazing place where parents and children could have fun together, and so, by July 17, 1955, Disneyland opened.

2 Initially, Disneyland cost one dollar for adults and 50 cents for 5 children to enter the park, and it was **(b)** park. Besides many rides and attractions, Disneyland had its own railroad because Walt Disney was a huge train **(c)**. Disneyland was also broadcast live on television, hosted by actor Ronald Reagan, and seen by almost 70 million Americans.

3 However, the opening of Disneyland was not as successful as Walt 10 Disney had hoped. Many **(d)** tickets were made so the park was **(e)**, while some rides broke or closed because of gas leaks. Yet, even with all the problems, Disneyland was a success as almost 500,000 people came to the park in the first month. The popularity of Disneyland was so great that in 1971, the bigger and more magical Disneyworld opened to the 15 public.

Comprehension Questions

Choose the best answer (a-c).

1. Why did Walt Disney want to build an amusement park?

   a. Because he liked trains very much

   b. Because he wanted families to have fun together

   c. Because it was an ideal place to show his cartoons

2. When did Disneyland open?

   a. In 1955

   b. In 1960

   c. In 1971

3. How much did it cost children to enter Disneyland when it first opened?

   a. $0.50

   b. $1

   c. $1.50

4. Why did Disneyland have its own train?

   a. Because it was too big to walk the entire park

   b. Because no other park had a train at the time

   c. Because Walt Disney loved trains

5. Who hosted the television broadcast of the opening of Disneyland?

   a. Walt Disney

   b. Ronald Reagan

   c. Ub Iwerks

6. How many people watched the opening of Disneyland on television?

   a. 500,000

   b. 7 million

   c. 70 million

7. Which of the following is NOT one of the problems Disneyland had on opening day?

   a. Gas leaks

   b. Too many people

   c. Rides and attractions were not fun

T/F Questions

Circle T or F for each of the following statements.

1. Disneyland was built before Disneyworld. (**T** / **F**)

2. More than 1 million people visited Disneyland in the first month after it opened.
   (**T** / **F**)

3. Disneyworld is much bigger than Disneyland. (**T** / **F**)

Writing Questions

Make a full sentence, using the following words.

1. Disneyland was (and / broadcast / television / by / hosted / on / live) actor
   Ronald Reagan.

   _____

2. However, the opening of Disneyland was (hoped / as / as / not / had / Walt
   Disney / successful).

   _____

Historic Route 66

国道 66 号線

> 多くの映画や音楽に出てくる国道 66 号線は、1926 年の開通時は 800 マイル（約 1,280km）しか舗装されていませんでした。1930 年代に、何千人もの職を求める青年たちが、道路の舗装を終えるため働かされ、その距離をのばしていったのです。

Reading 1 ▶ **Warm-up**

Using your dictionary, find the meanings of the following words.

1. route **2.** heritage **3.** merchant **4.** coined

5. migrate **6.** inspire **7.** pastime **8.** firsthand

Choose the best answer (a-c).

1. What do you imagine driving across America would be like?

   a. Very long and tiring

   b. An amazing experience

   c. No one does it

2. What does the word "nostalgia" mean?

   a. To think happily about past experiences

   b. To feel sad about historical events

   c. To think about the future

Reading 1 — A Symbol of Freedom & Mobility

🔊 Audio 24

1 Historic Route 66 had long been an experience of a lifetime for car buffs and travelers alike. While officially it does not exist anymore, the majority of the same route and original road across eight states from Chicago to Los Angeles can still be driven today.

2 Route 66, from 1926 to 1985, represents America's heritage and 5 tradition of freedom and mobility. Route 66 connected local merchants and farmers with new customers and business from the rest of America, which led to it being called the "Main Street of America." This had an immediate impact on towns and small communities alike, as cafes, restaurants, tourist attractions, and motels popped up along the 3,940 10 kilometers of highway.

3 During the *Great Depression* in the 1930's, novelist John Steinbeck coined the name "Mother Road" for Route 66, as the highway helped more than 200,000 people migrate across America to California to find jobs. Later, after World War II, thousands more Americans were 15 inspired to be mobile and move following Route 66. All of this led to the new great American pastime of the driving vacation.

4 Today, historic Route 66 still offers an unforgettable experience through America for those feeling nostalgic for the "good old days," interested in its history or those simply looking to experience it firsthand 20 for themselves. Following the old Route 66 is a beautiful drive that goes from the sunshine of California, past the Grand Canyon and Native American lands in the Southwest, through the heartlands of America, and on to the city streets of Chicago.

NOTES
l. 6: **mobility** 動きやすさ、移動性　l. 9: **immediate impact on** ～に与える直接の影響　l. 10: **pop up** 現れる　l. 23: **heartland** 中心地

Comprehension Questions

Choose the best answer (a-c).

1. How many U.S. states does Route 66 cross?

   a. 6 states

   b. 8 states

   c. 10 states

2. How long is the history of Route 66?

   a. From 1930-1966

   b. From 1926-1985

   c. From 1966-2000

3. Why was Route 66 important to so many people?

   a. Because it connected local farmers and businesses with new customers

   b. Because it was the easiest highway to drive

   c. Because it created new jobs for many people

4. How many kilometers long was the original Route 66?

   a. 66 km long

   b. 1,926 km long

   c. 3,940 km long

5. Why did novelist John Steinbeck call Route 66 the "Mother Road" during the Great Depression?

   a. Because many restaurants and tourist attractions started during this time

   b. Because it was the biggest and best highway to use in the entire United States

   c. Because it helped many people travel across America to find jobs they needed

6. What did Route 66 do to America after World War II?

   a. It created more business from Los Angeles to Chicago.

   b. It motivated Americans to get in their cars and drive more.

   c. It helped many Americans find new homes anywhere in America.

7. What is NOT one of the things you can experience when driving the old Route 66?

   a. The Grand Canyon

   b. Tourist attractions

   c. The Statue of Liberty

T/F Questions

Circle T or F for each of the following statements.

1. The entire Route 66 still exists and can be driven today. (**T** / **F**)

2. Route 66 is also known by two other names. (**T** / **F**)

3. Route 66 helped more than 200,000 people find a better life during the Great Depression. (**T** / **F**)

Writing Questions

Make a full sentence, using the following words.

1. Historic Route 66 (an / had / long / been / of / experience) a lifetime for car buffs and travelers alike.

_____

2. (on / had / Route 66 / impact / an / immediate) towns and small communities alike.

_____

© Steve Lagreca / Shutterstock.com

Listen to the following "Reading 2." Fill in the correct word or phrase in each blank (a-e) and match the definitions below.

a. _____   b. _____   c. _____

d. _____   e. _____

1. a publicly display

2. more than enough

3. giving a feeling of comfort

4. an object or part of a scenery that is easily recognized

5. to describe the unique nature of something

6. to design buildings

7. to be motivated

Reading 2 ▶ Tourist Attractions of Route 66

1 Historic Route 66 still provides a fantastic road trip through iconic American history. Along the journey there are **(a)** sights to see, from old-fashioned diners to the most famous American **(b)**.

2 Starting in Springfield, Illinois, the Cozy Dog Drive-in has a long
5 history with Route 66. It also claims to have created the corn dog back in the 1940s, which they called a Cozy Dog.

3 In Galena, Kansas, a 1930s era gas station sits with an old, rusty truck next to it. Route 66 and the old truck were part of the **(c)** for the 2006 Pixar movie, *Cars*, along with the truck character, Tow Mater.

10 **4** While in Texas, Cadillac Ranch is a must-see Route 66 attraction. This art exhibit of colorfully painted cars half-buried in the ground, has **(d)** American pop culture over the years through music and films.

5 In Amboy, California, is the iconic Roy's Motel & Café. Its 1950s futuristic style **(e)** called "Googie" can still be seen today with the
15 "Welcome to Fabulous Las Vegas." Finally, the journey along Route 66 ends at Santa Monica Pier.

NOTES
l. 5: **corn dog** アメリカンドッグ〔アメリカンドッグは和製英語〕　l. 7: **rusty** 色あせた

Comprehension Questions

Choose the best answer (a-c).

1. When did Cozy Dogs claim to have invented the corn dog?

    a. In the 1930s

    b. In the 1940s

    c. In the 1950s

2. Where can Cozy Dog be found?

    a. In Texas

    b. In Illinois

    c. In California

3. Why was Route 66 and the gas station in Galena made popular again in 2006?

    a. They were both on a popular U.S. TV show

    b. They were the ideas for a popular Pixar movie

    c. They encouraged more Americans to take a journey along Route 66

4. Which popular *Cars* character was created based on the Galena gas station truck?

    a. James P. Sullivan Truck

    b. Doc Hudson

    c. Tow Mater

5. What is the art exhibit that can be found on Route 66 in Texas?

    a. Colorfully painted row of cars

    b. A beautiful 1950s Cadillac

    c. Brightly colored architecture

6. What makes the art exhibit so important to travelers?

    a. It is the oldest landmark on Route 66.

    b. It is part of America's pop culture.

    c. Travelers feel it's the most iconic tourist attraction.

7. Where can you still see the 1950s futuristic architecture made famous by Roy's Motel & Café?

    a. In Santa Monica

    b. In Las Vegas

    c. In Kansas

T/F Questions

Circle T or F for each of the following statements.

1. Driving Route 66 is a good way to experience American history. (**T** / **F**)

2. The type of futuristic architecture from Roy's Motel & Café is called, "Google." (**T** / **F**)

3. Route 66 ends at Manhattan Beach Pier in California. (**T** / **F**)

Writing Questions

Make a full sentence, using the following words.

1. Along the journey (to / there / plenty / sights / are / of) see from old-fashioned diners to the most famous American landmarks.

   _____

2. Route 66 and an old truck (the / for / inspiration / of / were / part) a 2006 Pixar movie.

   _____

© a katz / Shutterstock.com

Chapter *13*

American Fast Food

ファストフード

" 米国では、ファストフード店で毎日食事をする人はなんと約 5,000 万人いることを知っていましたか？ 実際米国のファストフード産業は、年間約 1,000 億ドルを稼ぐ巨大産業であり、過去 15 年間その人気は衰えを見せていないのです。"

Reading 1 ▶ **Warm-up**

Using your dictionary, find the meanings of the following words.

1. inception   **2.** impressively   **3.** chain   **4.** establish

5. volume   **6.** eatery   **7.** carhop   **8.** ensure

Choose the best answer (a-c).

1. What do you imagine the first fast food restaurants in America were like?

   a. They were similar to today

   b. They were created for people in cars

   c. No one knows

2. What does the phrase "to be inspired" mean?

   a. To reuse something old

   b. To feel something new

   c. To get an idea to do something from a person or thing

Reading 1   The Invention of the Drive-in

🔊 Audio 26

1 The inception of fast food really began with America's new mobile and on-the-go lifestyle inspired by Route 66 and other highway systems built in the 1950s and 1960s, but the history of the hamburger itself is much older.

5 **2** Impressively, the first hamburger chain in the States was established in 1921, and it was not McDonald's. In Wichita, Kansas, Billy Ingram and Walter Anderson had success selling a high volume of cheap hamburgers at their restaurant called White Castle.

3 As cars became more popular and part of everyone's daily life,
10 restaurants began serving quick meals to customers straight to their cars. The drive-in concept was first popularized by a Texas eatery called the Pig Stand. Customers would park their cars and immediately be greeted by carhops. By the 1940s, carhops wore roller skates so they could deliver meals more quickly. They would serve burgers and fries on
15 a tray that would hook onto a car window. By 1948, McDonald's opened their fast-food chains, while Taco Bell and Burger King opened in the 1950s, and later on Wendy's began in 1969.

4 The eating habits of Americans were further changed by a California restaurant in 1948 that promised customers "no delay" as they were the
20 first eatery to establish the real drive-thru experience. With its clever name, In-N-Out, the restaurant lacked both inside seating and outside parking. This encouraged customers to order their meals from their cars through an intercom system and pick up their food directly from a takeout window.

25 **5** The start of drive-thrus ensured that fast food restaurants would continue to serve food like hamburgers and fries even to this day.

NOTES   l. 2: **on-the-go** 活動的な   l. 13: **greet** 出迎える   l. 23: **intercom** インターホン〔インターホンは和製英語〕
l. 22: **encourage** *someone* **to ~** 〔人〕に~することを促す

Comprehension Questions

Choose the best answer (a-c).

1. How did the idea of fast food first begin?

    a. It began because it was cheaper to do.

    b. It began because of America's new lifestyle.

    c. It began because Americans loved hotdogs.

2. What was the first hamburger chain in the States?

    a. McDonald's

    b. In-N-Out

    c. White Castle

3. What year was the first fast food chain established?

    a. In 1921

    b. In 1940

    c. In 1948

4. Which fast food chain is credited with having the first drive-in?

    a. In-N-Out

    b. White Castle

    c. Pig Stand

5. How did drive-ins work?

    a. People ordered food inside the restaurant and ate it in their cars.

    b. People ordered food from their cars and drove home.

    c. People ordered food from their cars and ate it in their cars.

6. What happened in 1948 that changed America's eating habits?

    a. Restaurants stopped using drive-ins

    b. McDonald's opened for the first time

    c. The first drive-thru restaurant opened

7. Where was the first drive-thru established?

    a. In Texas

    b. In Kansas

    c. In California

T/F Questions

Circle T or F for each of the following statements.

1. Billy Ingram and Walter Anderson are the owners of the Pig Stand. (**T** / **F**)

2. At drive-in restaurants, customers could order and eat directly from their cars.
(**T** / **F**)

3. In-N-Out promised customers "no delays" so they could eat quickly. (**T** / **F**)

Writing Questions

Make a full sentence, using the following words.

1. Customers would park their cars (immediately / carhops / and / by / greeted / be).

   _____

2. This encouraged customers (meals / their / their / from / order / to / cars)
   through an intercom system.

   _____

© junpinzon / Shutterstock.com

Reading 2 **Listening** 🔊 **Audio 27**

> Listen to the following "Reading 2." Fill in the correct word or phrase in each blank (a-e) and match the definitions below.

a. _____ b. _____ c. _____

d. _____ e. _____

1. something very foolish or unbelievable
2. as good as or better than others
3. an extraordinary person or thing
4. an event in which people compete
5. to exercise control over
6. a person who watches at a show, game, or other event
7. to be related to something

Reading 2   An American Tradition

1 There is nothing more American than eating hot dogs on Independence Day. Especially, eating competitively each year at Nathan's Famous Hot Dog Eating Contest.

2 Every year since 1972, thousands of **(a)** come to Coney Island, New York to eat hotdogs and watch this fun, but **(b)** event, which has become 5 **(c)** with the Fourth of July. It's even televised with over a million Americans tuning in to watch.

3 The yearly event has even become an internationally popular **(d)**. Until 1996, every contest was won by an American, except in 1984 when German, Birgit Felden won. Then, for the next decade until 2007, the 10 contest was **(e)** Japanese stars, Hirofumi Nakajima, Kazutoyo Arai, and fan favorite, Takeru Kobayashi, who won from 2001 to 2006. A women's division was also added in 2011.

4 Today, the Independence Day tradition has been dominated by 13-time winner, Joey Chestnut, who holds the record for eating 75 hot dogs 15 in ten minutes.

NOTES   l. 2: **competitively** 対抗意識をもって   l. 2: **Nathan's** ニューヨークに本社のある、ホットドッグを専門としたファストフード店を展開する企業。

Comprehension Questions

1. When is the famous hot dog eating contest held?

    a. On the 4th of July

    b. Every 4th month of the year

    c. Once a year

2. Where does the traditional event take place?

    a. In Las Vegas, Nevada

    b. In Long Island, New York

    c. In Los Angeles, California

3. How long has the popular event taken place?

    a. Since 1972

    b. Since 1982

    c. Since 1996

4. How many people watch the eating contest on television?

    a. Thousands of people

    b. Over a million people

    c. Hundreds of people

5. Who was the first non-American to win the contest?

    a. Hirofumi Nakajima

    b. Birgit Felden

    c. Joey Chestnut

6. Which Japanese star is the most successful contestant?

    a. Kazutoyo Arai

    b. Hirofumi Nakajima

    c. Takeru Kobayashi

7. What is the record for the number of hot dogs eaten in ten minutes?

    a. 71 hot dogs

    b. 72 hot dogs

    c. 75 hot dogs

T/F Questions

1. A separate women's division for the hot dog eating contest started in 2007. (**T** / **F**)

2. Joey Chestnut is an 11-time winner of the hot dog eating contest. (**T** / **F**)

3. Joey Chestnut is the current record holder for total number of hot dogs eaten in the contest. (**T** / **F**)

Writing Questions

Make a full sentence, using the following words.

1. (more / nothing / is / American / than / there) eating hot dogs on Independence Day.

   _____

2. The Independence Day hotdog eating (by / tradition / been / has / dominated) 13-time winner, Joey Chestnut.

   _____

© Michael Vi / Shutterstock.com

Google

グーグル

> 米国の主要企業（GAFAM*）の一つである Google 社。Google 社の
> 創設者が運用初期に使っていたストレージシステムは、当時最大サイズで
> あった 4GB のハードディスク 10 枚をレゴブロックで作った棚におさめた
> ものでした。 *Google. Amazon, Facebook, Apple, and Microsoft

Reading 1 ▶ **Warm-up**

Using your dictionary, find the meanings of the following words.

1. intrigue **2.** vast **3.** initially **4.** incorporate

5. progress **6.** derive **7.** signify **8.** prominent

Choose the best answer (a-c).

1. What do you imagine Google was like when it first started?

    a. It was a serious tech company.

    b. It started out small.

    c. It was similar to today.

2. What does the word "revolutionary" mean?

    a. To begin something new

    b. To cause a big change

    c. To imagine something big

Reading 1   Where It All Started

🔊 Audio 28

1 The origin story of Google dates all the way back to 1995, when Larry Page and Sergey Brin first met at Stanford University in California. Page was thinking about graduate school at Stanford and Brin was already a student who was, by chance, given the job of showing Page the university. 5

2 Their partnership began out of their intrigue over the vast amounts of data on the Internet, and how they could organize it all by importance. Thus, from their dormitory rooms at Stanford, they began working on their first type of search technology, which they initially called BackRub.

3 Through their continued work, Brin and Page incorporated the total 10 number of links associated with websites into their search engine. This helped people because websites with more related links would be more valuable, and those websites would go to the top of the search results. As their work progressed, they also renamed their search engine, too, and the new name Google was established. The name derives from the 15 mathematical number expression, *googol*, which equates to the number 1 followed by 100 zeros. Brin and Page wanted the new name to signify their goal of trying to organize all data in the world so it would be accessible and understandable for everyone.

4 Over the next few years, the revolutionary search engine, Google, 20 became more prominent, not only for students, but also in Silicon Valley, the tech capital of the world. In 1998, with an initial investment of $100,000 from Sun Microsystem's co-founder Andy Bechtolsheim, Google Inc. officially started.

NOTES   l. 3: **graduate school** 大学院   l. 8: **dormitory** 寮   ll.16-17: **the number 1 followed by 100 zeros** 数字の1に0が100 続く→ 10の100 乗   l. 22: **investment** 出資

Comprehension Questions

Choose the best answer (a-c).

1. What year did Larry Page and Sergey Brin first meet?

   a. In 1985

   b. In 1995

   c. In 1998

2. How did Page and Brin first meet?

   a. Page showed Brin around Stanford University.

   b. Brin showed Page around Stanford University.

   c. Both Brin and Page met in a class at Stanford University.

3. Why did Page and Brin start their partnership?

   a. Because they both lived together in a Stanford dormitory

   b. Because they both wanted to work for Google

   c. Because they both were interested in data and the Internet

4. What was the name of Page and Brin's first search engine?

   a. Backspace

   b. Google

   c. BackRub

5. What made Page and Brin's search engine so helpful?

   a. The useless websites were found quickly.

   b. The most valuable websites were listed first.

   c. Only the least popular websites were listed.

6. Why did Page and Brin rename their search engine to Google?

   a. Because the name better matched their own goals for organizing data on the Internet

   b. Because they got paid money to change their name

   c. Because they wanted the name Googol first, but couldn't, so they chose a similar name

7. What is the inspiration behind the name Google?

   a. Page and Brin wanted to have a fun name.

   b. It comes from a mathematical number expression.

   c. Sun Microsystems recommended the name.

T/F Questions

Chapter 14: Google

Circle T or F for each of the following statements.

1. Google, as a company, officially started in 1998. (**T** / **F**)

2. Sun Microsystem's co-founder Andy Bechtolsheim invested $10,000 into Google. (**T** / **F**)

3. Companies in the tech capital of the world, Silicon Valley, were not interested in Google. (**T** / **F**)

Writing Questions

Make a full sentence, using the following words.

1. Through their continued work, Brin and Page (number / incorporated / links / the / to / of) websites into their search engine.

   _____

2. As their work progressed, (engine / they / renamed / also / search / their / , too), and the new name Google was established.

   _____

© Uladzik Kryhin / Shutterstock.com

Reading 2 **Listening** 🔊 Audio 29

Listen to the following "Reading 2." Fill in the correct word or phrase in each blank (a-e) and match the definitions below.

a. _____ b. _____ c. _____

d. _____ e. _____

1. to be a person or persons who start a company
2. to go from place to place
3. to be recognized by many people
4. to have a common image or idea of a person or thing
5. to search for information
6. a belief or opinion that is held about a person or thing
7. to stop living in a particular place

Reading 2   **Fun Facts About Google**

1 Being one of the biggest and most **(a)** companies in the world means Google has many amazing stories to tell.

2 Google **(b)** started like many other new companies in Silicon Valley. Google started in a garage of a house that Page and Brin rented after
5 moving out of their dormitories. Years later, Google bought the house it started in because of its special memories for the **(c)**.

3 Google also has a **(d)** as a fun company. For example, in 2004, Google introduced Gmail on April 1st, which is April Fool's Day, so many people thought the announcement was fake news. Additionally, one of its
10 earliest "employees" was a sociable dog named Yoshka, as Google has always been a dog-friendly company. Later on, after the Googleplex campus opened in 2007, Google provided brightly colored bicycles called, "gBikes" that employees could use to **(e)** the two-mile long complex.

4 If you are thinking about how many more great stories are there
15 about Google, you should try googling it!

NOTES   l. 13: **complex** 総合施設   l. 15: **googling** 世間に非常に浸透している企業や商品名を動詞として使うことがある〔e.g. Tweet: ツイッターでつぶやく、Photoshop: 写真加工する、Xerox: コピーをとる〕

Comprehension Questions

Choose the best answer (a-c).

1. Where was Google's first "office" space?

   a. In a Silicon Valley office building

   b. In a small garage of a house

   c. At Stanford University

2. What did founders Page and Brin do with Google's first office space years later?

   a. They rented it out to new companies.

   b. They turned it into the new Googleplex.

   c. They bought it to keep it.

3. Which is NOT what Google is known for?

   a. Being serious

   b. Being a tech leader

   c. Being pet-friendly

4. Who was one of Google's first "employees"?

   a. Page and Brin's dormitory roommate from Stanford

   b. Page and Brin's friend from Silicon Valley, Andy Bechtolsheim

   c. A sociable dog

5. What year did Google open its campus, Googleplex?

   a. In 2004

   b. In 2007

   c. In 2014

6. Why did Google provide "gBikes" for employees to borrow?

   a. Because it was a fun way for employees to come to work

   b. Because Google wanted healthy employees

   c. Because the new Googleplex campus was so big

7. Why did most people not believe Gmail was real?

   a. Because Google didn't advertise it well

   b. Because it was announced on April 1st

   c. Because other companies said fake news about it

T/F Questions

Circle T or F for each of the following statements.

1. Google is one of the biggest companies in the world. (**T** / **F**)

2. The name of the famous dog at Google is Tashka. (**T** / **F**)

3. Google first introduced Gmail in 2005. (**T** / **F**)

Writing Questions

Make a full sentence, using the following words.

1. Being that it is one of the biggest and most well-known companies in the world, Google (tell / amazing / many / stories / has / to).

   _____

2. Googling is the best way to learn (how / stories / more / about / many / great) there are about Google.

   _____

© Juan Camilo Bernal / Shutterstock.com

Chapter *15*

The X Games

X ゲーム

> エクストリームスポーツ（X スポーツ）を知っていますか？　どのスポーツが X スポーツにあたるか明確な定義がないにもかかわらず、危険であることや、アスリートに興奮を与えることなど、いくつかの条件があります。たとえば観客を魅了するスノーボードは含まれるのでしょうか？

Reading 1 ▶ **Warm-up**

Using your dictionary, find the meanings of the following words.

1. competition　　2. attract　　3. claim　　4. draw

5. influential　　6. version　　7. promote　　8. mainstream

Choose the best answer (a-c).

1. What does the word "extreme" mean?
   a. thrilling
   b. safe
   c. unbelievable

2. What do you imagine the first competitions in the X Games were like?
   a. Very boring to watch
   b. Very exciting to watch
   c. Similar to today

1 The X Games is an entertaining competition of exciting and risky sports. It takes place twice a year during summer and winter. Many athletes from around the world come to compete for cash prizes and for gold, silver, and bronze medals, but also to claim the title as the best in
5 their sport.

2 The origin of the X Games is an interesting story. The ESPN sports network created the competition to attract young fans and athletes of Generation X. Additionally, the letter X is short for "extreme" which made the games a unique and influential sporting event.

10 **3** In 1995, the first Summer X Games was held in Rhode Island and included events in skateboarding, BMX biking, and motorcycling, among many others. The inaugural event was an instant success and drew more than 200,000 sports fans. There are also many famous stars now from the Summer X Games, but none more so than Bob Burnquist from
15 Brazil. Bob participated in the first games and retired in 2017, but holds the record for most medals ever won with 30.

4 The winter version of the X Games was held in 1997. Importantly, like the Summer X Games, the introduction of events like snowboarding, skiing, and snowmobiling have since helped promote these sports
20 globally. Snowboarding was added first to the 1998 Nagano Olympics, while years later, skier X, also known as ski cross, where athletes race head-to-head, was introduced at the Winter Olympics in 2010 in Vancouver, Canada.

5 Over the past 25 years, the X Games have helped sports like
25 skateboarding and snowboarding become mainstream around the world, and the annual competition only gets better every year.

NOTES
l. 2: **take place** 開催する

Comprehension Questions

Choose the best answer (a-c).

1. How often are the X Games held?

   a. Every two years

   b. Two times a year

   c. Every three years

2. Which is NOT a meaning for the 'X' in X Games?

   a. Extreme

   b. Generation X

   c. Non-professional sport

3. What year was the very first X Games?

   a. In 1995

   b. In 1997

   c. In 1998

4. Where was the first X Games held?

   a. Vancouver

   b. Nagano

   c. Rhode Island

5. How many total medals does the X Games record holder Bob Burnquist have?

   a. He has 13.

   b. He has 20.

   c. He has 30.

6. What Winter X event was NOT introduced to the Olympics?

   a. Snowboarding

   b. Snowmobiling

   c. Ski cross

7. How long has the X Games been around?

   a. For 15 years

   b. For 20 years

   c. For 25 years

T/F Questions

Circle T or F for each of the following statements.

1. The first X Games was viewed by 100,000 fans. (**T** / **F**)

2. Skateboarder Bob Burnquist is from the USA. (**T** / **F**)

3. The X Games have helped many sports become more popular around the world.
(**T** / **F**)

Writing Questions

Make a full sentence, using the following words.

1. Many athletes (from / for / around / compete / to / come / the world) cash
prizes and for gold, silver, and bronze medals.

   _____

2. There are also many famous stars now from the Summer X Games, (Bob
Burnquist / so / none / but / more / than).

   _____

Reading 2 ▶ **Listening**

🔊 **Audio 31**

> Listen to the following "Reading 2." Fill in the correct word or phrase in each blank (a-e) and match the definitions below.

a. _____ b. _____ c. _____

d. _____ e. _____

1. to encourage or motivate others to do something
2. ever
3. to be delayed
4. to hang loosely
5. to happen immediately
6. unexceptional
7. to become more popular than usual

Reading 2   Shaun White

1 Shaun White is probably the best-known extreme sports athlete in the world and has been an **(a)** on many young boys and girls.

2 White started snowboarding at only six years old and was an **(b)** phenomenon. He won his first competition a year later and five more national titles before turning pro at just thirteen years old. ⁵

3 He participated in his first Winter X Games in 2000 and has currently won 18 total medals in the superpipe and slopestyle events, which is the second best **(c)**. White has also had success at the Olympics, too. At the Turin Olympics in 2006, he won the first of a record three gold medals for snowboarding, while also earning his famous nickname, "The Flying ¹⁰ Tomato," because of his **(d)**, bright red hair.

4 White is also a professional skateboarder, turning pro at seventeen. He is also the only athlete to ever win gold medals in both the Summer and Winter X Games. His 15 gold medals are also a record for the most ever won at both X Games. White's success in both skateboarding and ¹⁵ snowboarding has **(e)** both sports and also makes Shaun White the greatest of all time.

NOTES
l. 11: **bright** 明るい

Comprehension Questions

1. When did Shaun White start snowboarding?

    a. At age six

    b. At age eight

    c. At age thirteen

2. How many national championship did Shaun White win before he became a professional snowboarder?

    a. He won one national championship.

    b. He won three national championships.

    c. He won five national championships.

3. When did Shaun White first participate in the X Games?

    a. In 1998

    b. In 2000

    c. In 2006

4. How successful has Shaun White been in the Winter X Games?

    a. He has won 15 total medals.

    b. He has participated in 15 Winter X Games.

    c. He has the second most total medals in Winter X Games' history.

5. Where did Shaun White get his famous nickname?

    a. At the Winter X Games

    b. At the Summer X Games

    c. At the Turin Olympics

6. Which is NOT one of Shaun White's records?

    a. Three gold medals in the Olympics

    b. Three gold medals in skateboarding

    c. Fifteen gold medals in the X Games

7. What is Shaun White's special achievement in extreme sports?

    a. He is the only athlete to win gold medals at both the Winter and Summer X Games.

    b. He is the only athlete to win gold medals at the X Games and Olympics.

    c. He is the only athlete to do both snowboarding and skateboarding.

T/F Questions

Circle T or F for each of the following statements.

1. Shaun White turned professional in snowboarding at age thirteen. (**T** / **F**)

2. Shaun White's nickname is the "Floppy Tomato." (**T** / **F**)

3. Shaun White was a professional skateboarder before snowboarding. (**T** / **F**)

Writing Questions

Make a full sentence, using the following words.

1. Shaun White is probably the best-known extreme sport athlete in the world (and / an / to / inspiration / young / many) boys and girls.

   _____

2. White's success in both skateboarding and snowboarding has elevated both sports and also makes (of / the / all / greatest / Shaun White / time).

   _____

Chapter 15: The X Games

Modern America: Culture, Society and History
現代米国の文化・社会・歴史

2021 年 4 月 5 日　初版第 1 刷発行
2024 年 4 月 10 日　初版第 3 刷発行

著　　者　Ryan Smithers ／ Craig Gamble

発 行 者　森　信久
発 行 所　株式会社　松 柏 社
　　　　　〒102−0072　東京都千代田区飯田橋 1 − 6 − 1
　　　　　TEL　03 (3230) 4813（代表）
　　　　　FAX　03 (3230) 4857
　　　　　http://www.shohakusha.com
　　　　　e-mail: info@shohakusha.com

装　　幀　小島トシノブ（NONdesign）
組　　版　木野内宏行（ALIUS）
印刷・製本　シナノ書籍印刷株式会社

略号 = 768
ISBN978-4-88198-768-1
Copyright © 2021 Ryan Smithers and Craig Gamble